THE DIDSBURY LECTURES ARE
DELIVERED ANNUALLY AT
THE NAZARENE THEOLOGICAL COLLEGE,
MANCHESTER, U.K., BY LEADING SCHOLARS FROM
A VARIETY OF SCHOOLS OF THOUGHT.

LECTURERS HAVE INCLUDED JAMES ATKINSON, C. K. BARRETT,
PAUL BASSETT, F. F. BRUCE, RONALD E. CLEMENTS, DAVID J. A. CLINES,
ALEX R. G. DEASLEY, JAMES D. G. DUNN, R. T. FRANCE,
COLIN E. GUNTON, DONALD GUTHRIE, MORNA D. HOOKER,
I. HOWARD MARSHALL, A. SKEVINGTON-WOOD,
JAMES B. TORRANCE, THOMAS F. TORRANCE
AND ANDREW F. WALLS.

WORSHIP, COMMUNITY & THE TRIUNE GOD OF GRACE

JAMES B. TORRANCE

InterVarsity Press
Downers Grove, Illinois

Published in the United States of America by InterVarsity Press, Downers Grove, Illinois, with permission from Paternoster Press, Carlisle, U.K.

InterVarsity Press® is the book-publishing division of InterVarsity Christian Fellowship®, a student movement active on campus at hundreds of universities, colleges and schools of nursing in the United States of America, and a member movement of the International Fellowship of Evangelical Students. For information about local and regional activities, write Public Relations Dept., InterVarsity Christian Fellowship, 6400 Schroeder Rd., P.O. Box 7895, Madison, WI 53707-7895.

Cover photograph: SuperStock, Jacksonville, FL.

ISBN 0-8308-1895-2

Printed in the United States of America ∞

Library of Congress Cataloging-in-Publication Data

Torrance, James.
      Worship, community & the triune God of grace/James B. Torrance.
            p.   cm.
      Originally published: Carlisle, U.K.: Paternoster Press, 1996.
      Includes bibliographical references.
      ISBN 0-8308-1895-2
      1. Public worship.   2. Trinity.   3. Grace (Theology)   4. Jesus
Christ—Priesthood.   5. Sacraments.   6. Analogy (Religion)
7. Sexism in liturgical language.   I. Title.
BV15.T67   1997
264-dc21

                                                                                            97-8456
                                                                                                  CIP

19   18   17   16   15   14   13   12   11   10   9   8   7   6   5   4   3   2   1

12   11   10   09   08   07   06   05   04   03   02   01   00   99   98   97

To my dear wife Mary
who has helped me to see the meaning
of being in loving communion
with God and one another

Preface

It was a unique privilege to be invited to give the Didsbury
Lectures in the Nazarene Theological College, Manchester, in
November 1994, on the theology of worship. I have long
thought and taught that the right road into Christian theology
is taken by reflecting on Christian worship in the light of the
Bible. The Bible is supremely a manual of worship, but too
often it has been treated, particularly in Protestantism, as a
manual of ethics, of moral values, of religious ideas, or even of
sound doctrine. When we see that the worship and mission of
the church are the gift of participating through the Holy Spirit
in the incarnate Son's communion with the Father and the
Son's mission from the Father to the world, that the unique
center of the Bible is Jesus Christ, "the apostle and high priest
whom we confess" (Heb 3:1), then the doctrines of the Trinity,
the incarnation, the atonement, the ministry of the Spirit,
Church and sacraments, our understanding of the kingdom,
our anthropology and eschatology, all unfold from that center.
If out of the confessional (kerygmatic) statements of the Bible

come doxological statements, Christian dogmatics unfolds
from reflection on doxology. True theology is done in the
presence of God in the midst of the worshiping community.
The "two horizons" of the Bible and our contemporary church
life fuse in worship, as at the Lord's Table, when we seek
together in a life of communion to comprehend with the saints
of all ages the triune love of God in Christ.

This is why it was a joy to offer these lectures in the Nazarene
Theological College, which is such a warm-hearted, believing,
worshiping community. The Wesleys sang their theology in
their hymns:

Veiled in flesh the Godhead see,
    Hail the incarnate Deity,
Pleased as man with man to dwell,
    Jesus, our Immanuel.

True theology is theology that sings. Commenting on the
words from Psalm 22:22 put into the lips of Jesus by the writer
to the Hebrews, "I will sing your praise in the great congregation" (2:12), Calvin says: "Christ is the great choirmaster who
tunes our hearts to sing God's praise."

These lectures seek to set out such an understanding of
worship. They are not a study in liturgics—the how to worship—nor in the history of the shape of the liturgy, important
as such disciplines are. They are based on the conviction that
how we worship God must reflect who God is—the triune God
of grace—and what he has done and is doing for us in Christ
and by the Holy Spirit. As offered here, they are a slightly
expanded form of the lectures I gave in Manchester, with an
introduction and an appendix on human language for God.
They incorporate material from lectures I have given in colleges
and summer schools in different countries in recent years, some
of which I have published in articles elsewhere: *The Forgotten*

Trinity in the British Council of Churches trilogy; on "The Place of Jesus Christ in Worship" in the *Church Service Society Annual* 1970, reprinted in *Theological Foundations for Ministry,* ed. Ray S. Anderson, 1979, T & T Clark and Eerdmans, also in "Doctrine and Practice of Public Worship in the Reformed Churches," the Report of the Committee on Public Worship and Aids to Devotion to the General Assembly of the Church of Scotland, 1971; and on "The Vicarious Humanity of Christ" in *The Incarnation,* ed. T. F. Torrance, 1981, Handsel Press. I see these lectures as a call to the church to live out of her true center in Jesus Christ.

Introduction

The Place of Jesus Christ in Worship

GOD HAS MADE ALL CREATURES FOR HIS GLORY. WITH-out knowing it, the lilies of the field in their beauty glorify God with a glory greater than that of Solomon, the sparrow on the housetop glorifies God, and the universe in its vastness and remoteness is the theater of God's glory. But God made men and women in his own image to be the priests of creation and to express on behalf of all creatures the praises of God, so that through human lips the heavens might declare the glory of God. When we, who know we are God's creatures, worship God together, we gather up the worship of all creation. Our chief end is to glorify God, and creation realizes its own creaturely glory in glorifying God through human lips.

But nature fails in its realization because of our human failure. Instead of singing songs of joy, the whole creation groans in universal travail, waiting for the fulfillment of God's purposes in human lives. Does God then abandon his purposes for humanity and for all his creatures? Does God leave all nature to be subject to vanity and futility—to be ruthlessly exploited and abused—and forget he has made us in his image for a life of communion and shared stewardship?

The good news is that God comes to us in Jesus to stand in for us and bring to fulfillment his purposes of worship and communion. Jesus comes to be the priest of creation to do for us, men and women, what we failed to do, to offer to the Father the worship and the praise we failed to offer, to glorify God by a life of perfect love and obedience, to be the one true servant of the Lord. In him and through him we are renewed by the Spirit in the image of God and in the worship of God in a life of shared communion. Jesus comes as our brother to be our great high priest, to carry on his loving heart the joys, the sorrows, the prayers, the conflicts of all his creatures, to reconcile all things to God, and to intercede for all nations as our eternal mediator and advocate. He comes to stand in for us in the presence of the Father, when in our failure and bewilderment we do not know how to pray as we ought to, or forget to pray altogether. By his Spirit he helps us in our infirmities.

As the head of all things, by whom and for whom all things were created, he makes us his body, and calls us to be a royal priesthood offering spiritual sacrifices. He calls us that we might be identified with him by the Spirit, not only in his communion with the Father, but also in his great priestly work and ministry of intercession, that our prayers on earth might be the echo of his prayers in heaven. Whatever else our worship is, it is our liturgical amen to the worship of Christ.

This is the "wonderful exchange" (*mirifica commutatio—admirabile commercium*) by which Christ takes what is ours (our broken lives and unworthy prayers), sanctifies them, offers them without spot or wrinkle to the Father, and gives them back to us, that we might "feed" upon him in thanksgiving. He takes our prayers and makes them his prayers, and he makes his prayers our prayers, and we know our prayers are heard "for Jesus' sake." This is life in the Spirit, worship understood in terms of *sola gratia*. This is the trinitarian nature of all true worship and communion.

Christian worship is, therefore, our participation through the Spirit in the Son's communion with the Father, in his vicarious life of worship and intercession. It is our response to our Father for all that he has done for us in Christ. It is our self-offering in body, mind and spirit, in response to the one true offering made for us in Christ, our response of gratitude (*eucharistia*) to God's grace (*charis*), our sharing by grace in the heavenly intercession of Christ. Therefore, anything we say about worship—the forms of worship, its practice and procedure—must be said in the light of him to whom it is a response. It must be said in the light of the gospel of grace. We must ask ourselves whether our forms of worship convey the gospel. Are they an appropriate response to the gospel? Do they help people to apprehend the worship and ministry of Christ as he draws us by the Spirit into a life of shared communion, or do they hinder? Do they make the real presence of Christ transparent in worship, or do they obscure it? To answer these questions, we have to look at the meaning, the content of worship, before we can decide whether our traditions and procedures are adequate. More profoundly, we have to consider our doctrine of God in worship. Is he the triune God of grace who has created us and redeemed us to participate freely in his life of communion and in his concerns for the world or is he the contract-God who has to be conditioned into being gracious by what *we* do—by our religion? If our worship is to be intelligent, meaningful worship, offered joyfully in the freedom of the Spirit, we must look at the realities which inspire us and demand from us an intelligent, meaningful response. So the apostle says in Romans 12:1—after expounding the gospel of grace in the first eleven chapters— "With eyes wide open to the mercies of God, I beg you, my brothers (and sisters), as an act of intelligent worship (*logike latreia*), to give him your bodies as a living sacrifice, consecrated to him and acceptable by him" (J. B. Phillips).

The writer of the Epistle to the Hebrews describes our Lord as the *Leitourgos* (Heb 8:2), "the leader of our worship," "the minister of the real sanctuary which the Lord pitched and not man." As such the *leitourgia* of Jesus is contrasted with the *leitourgia* of men and women. This is the worship which God has provided for humanity, and which alone is acceptable to God. In Old Testament Israel, the priests sought to fulfill their God-given ordinances of worship (*dikaiōmata latreias*), but their worship only foreshadowed the true worship and self-offering of Christ on our behalf. "But now Christ has come . . . and offered himself without blemish to God, a spiritual and eternal sacrifice, and his blood will cleanse our conscience from the deadness of our former ways and fit us for the service (*latreuein*) of the living God" (Heb 9:11-15; 10:1-25). Our risen and ascended Lord is still "the high priest over the house of God," the minister of the sanctuary, the one true worshiper who leads us in our worship. The worship of Christ thus gathers up the worship of Israel, replaces it, and is the substance of all Christian worship. So Calvin expounded it at the time of the Reformation in the *Institutes* 2.9-11ff. and 4.14-17, and also in his commentary on the epistle to the Hebrews. At the heart of his interpretation of baptism and the Lord's Supper, and of all worship, (1) Christ's baptism is our baptism—set forth in our water baptism—(2) Christ's sacrifice is our sacrifice—set forth at the table—and (3) Christ's worship is our worship—set forth in our worship and prayers. This is the heart of the Reformed doctrine of justification by grace, that Christ has become for us wisdom and righteousness and sanctification and redemption—that Christ's righteousness is our righteousness apprehended by faith.

It will be my concern in the following chapters to stress the need to recover this New Testament understanding of worship which recognizes that the real agent in all true worship is Jesus Christ. He is our great high priest and ascended Lord, the one true worshiper who unites us to himself by the Spirit in an act of memory and in a life of communion, as he lifts us up by word and sacrament into the very triune life of God. This is, therefore, not only the heart of our theology of the Lord's Supper but also of preaching. The Reformers spoke of the threefold office (*triplex munus*) of Christ as king, priest and prophet, and in these terms expounded not only the once and for all ministry of Christ, but also his continuing ministry. In our subsequent Protestant tradition we have stressed the continuing prophetic office of Christ in our very proper emphasis on preaching. We have also stressed the continuing kingship of Christ—"the crown rights of the Redeemer" as head over church and state—in confessing Jesus as Lord. He is King of kings and Lord of lords. But too often we have neglected the continuing priesthood of Christ, perhaps out of a negative reaction to rather Pelagian ways in which this has been interpreted in Roman Catholic and Anglo-Catholic theology. There a stress on the priesthood of the Church might be felt to obscure the sole priesthood of Christ and, therefore, the meaning of grace.

We can do the same with a one-sided stress on the priesthood of all (individual) believers. But it seems to me that we cannot have a true understanding of worship, prayer, baptism and the Lord's Supper without a New Testament understanding of the priesthood of Christ. It is he who calls the church into being as a royal priesthood to participate by grace in his continuing ministry, lifting us by the Spirit into the very triune life of God in wonderful communion.

Chapter One

Worship— Unitarian or Trinitarian?

AMONG THE CHRISTIAN CHURCHES, THERE ARE MANY forms of worship deriving from different traditions—Anglican, Presbyterian, Methodist, Baptist, Roman Catholic, Eastern Orthodox, Pentecostal. And within these there are wide varieties. Today many churches and Christian groups are experimenting, wondering what are meaningful and relevant forms of worship in the context of a changing secular world. The urgent question therefore arises, How we are to evaluate these many forms? What makes worship Christian in whatever form it takes? What is the place of Jesus Christ and the Holy Spirit in our worship and prayers to God our Father? As we reflect on the wide varieties of forms of worship among our Christian churches, it seems to me that, broadly speaking, we can discern two different views.[1]

Two Views of Worship

The unitarian view. Probably the most common and wide-spread view is that worship is something which we, religious people, do—mainly in church on Sunday. We go to church, we sing our psalms and hymns to God, we intercede for the world, we listen to the sermon (too often simply an exhortation), we offer our money, time and talents to God. No doubt we need God's grace to help us do it. We do it because Jesus taught us to do it and left us an example of how to do it. But worship is what *we* do before God.

In theological language, this means that the only priesthood is our priesthood, the only offering our offering, the only intercessions our intercessions.

Indeed this view of worship is in practice unitarian, has no doctrine of the mediator or sole priesthood of Christ, is human-centered, has no proper doctrine of the Holy Spirit, is too often non-sacramental, and can engender weariness. We sit in the pew watching the minister "doing his thing," exhorting us "to do our thing," until we go home thinking we have done our duty for another week! This kind of do-it-yourself-with-the-help-of-the-minister worship is what our forefathers would have called "legal worship" and not "evangelical worship"—what the ancient church would have called Arian or Pelagian and not truly catholic. It is not trinitarian. Bishop Lesslie Newbigin has commented that when the average Christian in this country hears the name of God, he or she does not think of the Trinity. After many years of missionary work in India among Eastern religions, he returned to find that much worship in the West is in practice, if not in theory, unitarian.

The trinitarian view. The second view of worship is that it is the gift of participating through the Spirit in the incarnate Son's communion with the Father. It means participating in union with Christ, in what he has done for us once and for all, in his self-offering to the Father, in his life and death on the cross. It also means participating in what he is continuing to do for us in the presence of the Father and in his mission from the Father to the world. There is only one true Priest through whom and with whom we draw near to God our Father. There is only one Mediator between God and humanity. There is only one offering which is truly acceptable to God, and it is not ours. It is the offering by which he has sanctified for all time those who come to God by him (Heb 2:11; 10:10, 14). There is only one who can lead us into the presence of the Father by his sacrifice on the cross. This is why the Reformers, in their critique of certain medieval concepts of priesthood, stressed the sole priesthood of Christ, and reinterpreted the church as a royal priesthood participating in the priesthood of Christ. Is not the bread which we break our sharing in the body of Christ, and the cup which we bless our sharing in the blood of Christ? Our sonship and communion with the Father, are they not our sharing by the Spirit of adoption in his Sonship and communion with the Father? Our intercessions and mission to the world, are they not the gift of participating in the intercessions and mission of "the apostle and high priest whom we confess" (Heb 3:1)? Our baptism, is it not the gift of participating through water and the Spirit in the One Baptism, Christ's baptism for us in the waters of Jordan and in blood upon the cross, which alone washes away our sins? Is this not the meaning of life in the Spirit, of that important New Testament word *koinōnia*, which can be translated "communion," "fellowship," "sharing," "participation"? "God has sent the Spirit of his Son into our hearts, crying,: "*Abba!* Father!" (Gal 4:6 RSV).

This view is trinitarian and incarnational. It takes seriously the New Testament teaching about the sole priesthood and headship of Christ, his self-offering for us to the Father and our life in union with Christ through the Spirit, with a vision of the Church as the body of Christ. It is fundamentally sacramental, but in a way which enshrines the gospel of grace—that God our Father, in the gift of his Son and the gift of the Spirit, gives us what he demands—the worship of our hearts and minds. He lifts us up out of ourselves to participate in the very life and communion of the Godhead, that life of communion for which we were created. This is the heart of our theology of the Eucharist, of Holy Communion. So we are baptized in the name of the Father, the Son and the Holy Spirit into the community, the one body of Christ, which confesses faith in the one God, Father, Son and Holy Spirit, and which worships the Father through the Son in the Spirit. We are baptized into a life of communion. The Christian doctrine of the Trinity is the grammar of this participatory understanding of worship and prayer.

This view is both catholic and evangelical. Whereas the first view can be divisive, in that every church and denomination "does its own thing" and worships God in its own way, the second is unifying. It recognizes that there is only one way to come to the Father, namely through Christ in the communion of the Spirit, in the communion of saints, whatever outward form our worship may take. If the first way can engender weariness, this second way, the way of grace, releases joy and ecstasy. With inward peace we are lifted up by the Spirit into the presence of the Father, into a life of wonderful communion, into a life of praise and adoration in union with Christ. We know that the living Christ is in our midst, leading our worship, our prayers and our praises.

It was the concern of the Reformers to recover this New Testament and early Christian view of worship. The medieval

Church had tended to substitute the priesthood, the sacrifice, the merits, the intercession of the church—the vicarious humanity of the *ecclesia* (Mary and the saints)—for the vicarious humanity of Christ in a way which obscured the gospel of grace, the good news of what God has done for us in Christ. The Reformers saw clearly the significance of the Pauline teaching about justification—that we are freely accepted by God in Christ, not because of our "good works," but by God's grace received in faith. They also saw clearly that God does not accept us because we have offered worthy worship. In his love, he accepts us freely in the person of his beloved Son. It is he who in our name and on our behalf, in our humanity, has made the one offering to the Father which alone is acceptable to God for all humanity, for all nations, for all times. It is he who unites us with himself in the one body, in his communion with the Father and in his continuing intercessions. The real agent in worship, in a New Testament understanding, is Jesus Christ who leads us in our praises and prayers, "the one true minister of the sanctuary," the *leitourgos ton hagion*, (Heb 8:1, 2). He is the High Priest who, by his one offering of himself for us on the cross, now leads us into the Holy of Holies, the holy presence of the Father, in holy communion.

Whereas the unitarian view is in reality destructive of the sacraments, the trinitarian view sees the Lord's Supper as the supreme expression of all worship. It is the act in which the risen and ascended Lord meets us at his table, in the power of the Spirit, to bring his passion to our remembrance and to draw us to himself that we may share his communion with the Father and his intercessions for the world.

One of my famous predecessors in the University of Aberdeen during the seventeenth century was Professor Henry Scougal, the author of the devotional classic *The Life of God in the Soul of Man*. This book had a profound influence on the rise of Methodism. George Whitfield, one of the founders of Methodism, tells us in his diary that it was the reading of this book which led to his conversion—the discovery that worship is not just something which we, religious people, do to please God, but that in worship Christ himself comes to live in our hearts by the Spirit and draws us into the very life of God. The title of the book might well have been "The life of humanity, lifted up into the very life of the triune God." John Wesley produced an edition of Scougal's work, which was studied in the Holy Club in Oxford. It is interesting to think that a Scottish Reformed Presbyterian theologian in Aberdeen had some influence on the rise of Methodism![2]

Three Theological Models Today

If this account of two views of worship in the church today is accurate, we must ask why we have drifted away from the trinitarian view of the great Greek Fathers for which the Reformers contended, into such a human-centered unitarian one. Could the dominance of the unitarian view of worship be one supreme reason why the doctrine of the Trinity has receded? If we take our eyes off Jesus Christ, the only one who can lead us by the Spirit into communion with the Father, do we not fall back on ourselves and our own religious efforts—with what Paul calls a false "confidence in the flesh" (Rom 10:3), that we can meet God's holy requirements, the *dikaiōmata* of the law?

Corresponding to these two different views of worship, we can discern three different contemporary theological models: the first avowedly unitarian, the second unitarian in tendency and practice, and only the third genuinely trinitarian.

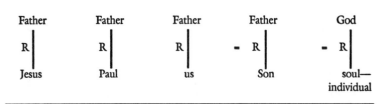

Figure 1. The Unitarian Model (Harnack, Hick—Liberal Protestantism)

Model 1: The Harnack (Hick) Model. The first model (see figure 1) is that of nineteenth-century Protestant liberalism, given classical expression by Adolf Harnack in his 1900 Berlin lectures *Das Wesen des Christentums,* or *What is Christianity?* Recently Professor John Hick has sought to revive it in an adapted form. According to this, the heart of religion is the soul's immediate relationship to God. What God the Father was to Old Testament Israel, he was to Jesus, and what he was to Jesus, he was to Paul and still is the same to us and all men and women today. We, with Jesus, stand as men and women, as brothers and sisters, worshiping the one Father but not worshiping any incarnate Son. Jesus is man but not God. We do not need any mediator, or "myth of God incarnate."

In Harnack's own words: "The Gospel, as Jesus proclaimed it, has to do with the Father only and not with the Son."[3] Jesus' purpose was to confront men and women with the Father, not with himself. He proclaimed the Fatherhood of God and the brotherhood of mankind, but not himself. "The Christian religion is something simple and sublime." It means "God and the soul, the soul and its God" and this, he says, must be kept "free from the intrusion of any alien element."[4] Nothing must come between the child and his heavenly Father, be it priest, or Bible, or law, or doctrine, or Jesus Christ himself! The major "alien element" which Harnack has in mind is belief in the incarnation, a doctrine which he regarded as emerging from the hellenizing of the simple message of Jesus.

This view is clearly unitarian and individualistic. The center of everything is our immediate relationship with God, our present-day experience. The Father-Son relationship is generic, not unique. With this interpretation, all the great dogmas of the church disappear:

□ The doctrine of the Trinity. We are all sons and daughters of God and the Spirit is the spirit of brotherly love.

□ The incarnation. Jesus Christ is not "his only (*unicus*) Son, our Lord," but one of the class of creaturely sons of God. Sonship is not unique to Christ.

□ The doctrines of the Spirit, union with Christ, the Church as the body of Christ and the sacraments. Jesus did not found a church. He proclaimed the kingdom of God as a fellowship of love.

This liberal reconstruction made deep inroads and accounts in measure for the moralistic view of Christianity—where Jesus is the teacher of ethical principles, and where the religious life is our attempt to follow the example of Jesus, living by the golden rule, "doing to others as you would be done by." With this moralistic, individualistic understanding of God and the Christian life, the doctrine of the Trinity loses its meaning, in fact disappears—and with it all doctrines of atonement and unconditional free grace, held out to us in Christ.

Model 2: The Existential, Present-day Experience Model. Here again faith means contemporary immediacy (see figure 2). God gives himself to us in grace in the present moment of encounter, and we respond in faith, in repentance and decision. The center is "God and me," today. But this response in faith is only made possible by the *work* of Christ on the cross.

According to this model, we are accepted by God as forgiven, as his children today, because of the death of Jesus on the cross

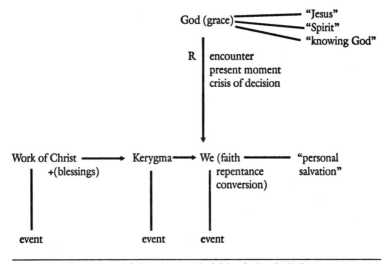

Figure 2. The Existential, Experience Model (early Barth, Bultmann, evangelical experience)

nineteen hundred years ago. The work of Jesus is instrumental in our present faith and experience of salvation. The event of the cross, through the event of preaching (the *kērygma*) gives rise to the event of faith. This can be interpreted in radical liberal (unitarian?) terms, as in Bultmann, or in more evangelical terms, as in the early Barth. For Bultmann, it is the event of the cross which through the *kērygma* gives rise to the self-understanding and authentic existence of faith. But this can apparently be asserted without any belief in the Trinity or the incarnation. For the early Barth, God in Christ, the living Word, meets us today in the crisis of decision, in the commitment of faith, on the ground of the atoning sacrifice of Jesus Christ on the cross. But this emphasis on the present moment of encounter can dehistoricize the gospel of the incarnation as Barth himself came to see, and as writers like D. M. Baillie in *God Was in Christ* were quick to show. Stressing the work of Christ at the expense of his person can reduce the gospel to "events" with no ontology (separate act and being) and make our religious experience of grace central. As Bonhoeffer saw, we are then more interested in the blessings of Christ than Jesus Christ himself. It is a failure not to recognize that salvation is not simply through the work of Christ (*per Christum*), but is primarily given to us in his person (*in Christo*). We draw near to God our Father in and through Christ, in the communion of the Spirit.

Once again, as in moralistic approaches to the gospel, in such a "theology of experience," the doctrine of the Trinity can recede and be regarded as metaphysical speculation which cannot be verified by religious experience. At best it may be a way of describing in metaphorical language God's relationship to the world and our experience, not what he is eternally in himself. As such it is Sabellian, as in Schleiermacher, and in practice unitarian. Indeed the latent or explicit unitarianism of this approach is what gave rise to Sabellianism in the early church, and often again in nineteenth-century theology. I think we see this clearly in much Anglo-Saxon Christianity, both liberal and evangelical, in its preoccupation with individual religious experience, subjectively interpreted. We can, therefore, understand why Karl Barth in his *Church Dogmatics*, in his avowed concern to give central place to Jesus Christ, the incarnate Lord, and to interpret *Christus pro nobis* as prior to *Christus in nobis*, dealt with the doctrine of the Trinity in his *Prolegomena* (1932). We can also understand why Bonhoeffer in his *Christology* criticized the attempt to reconstruct theology from the starting point of "religious experience," as pioneered by Schleiermacher, Ritschl, Herrmann, Harnack and Bousset. He pleaded for following the biblical pattern of giving priority to the question of *who* over *what* and *how*—that we interpret the atonement and personal faith in terms of the incarnation (the triune God of grace) and not the other way round. The pragmatic, problem-centered preoccupation with the question of *how* in our Western culture can so readily reduce the gospel to the category of means and ends. Bonhoeffer saw this in Ritschlian thought, and we see it often today in an over-concern for relevance. This culture Protestantism sees religion as the means to realize the ends of culture.

The existential model in its different forms seeks to do justice to *sola gratia, sola fide,* to "the form of the personal" (John Macmurray's phrase), but it is still too anthropologically centered. Although it stresses the God-humanward movement in Christ, the human-Godward movement is still ours! It emphasizes *our* faith, *our* decision, *our* response in an event theology which short-circuits the vicarious humanity of Christ and belittles union with Christ. For all that it may emphasize the vicarious work of Christ on the cross to bring forgiveness and make our faith a real human possibility, it fails to see the place of the high priesthood of Jesus Christ as the *leitourgos* (Heb 8:2). It is he who leads our worship, bears our sorrows on his heart and intercedes for us, presenting us to the Father in himself as God's dear children, and uniting us with himself in his life in the Spirit. To reduce worship to this two-dimensional thing—God and ourselves, today—is to imply that God throws us back upon ourselves to make our response. It ignores the fact that God has already provided for us that response which alone is acceptable to him—the offering made for the whole human race in the life, obedience and passion of Jesus Christ. But is this not to lose the comfort and the peace of the gospel, as well as the secret of true Christian prayer? The gift of sharing in the intercessions of Christ is that when we do not know how to pray as we ought, the Spirit makes intercession for us. Whatever else our faith is, it is a response to a response already

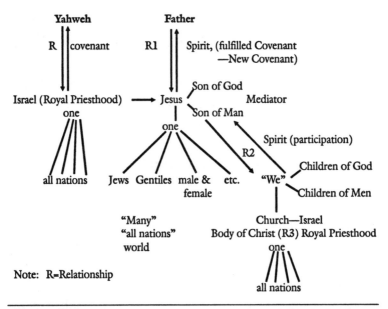

Figure 3. The Trinitarian, Incarnational Model (Nicaea, Calvin, McLeod Campbell, Barth)

made for us and continually being made for us in Christ, the pioneer of our faith.

Model 3: The Incarnational Trinitarian Model. This model (see figure 3) articulates the trinitarian view of worship—that worship is the gift of participating through the Spirit in the incarnate Son's communion with the Father. Indeed, we have suggested that the doctrine of the Trinity is the grammar of this view of worship and prayer.

At the center of the New Testament stands not our religious experience, not our faith or repentance or decision, however important these are, but a unique relationship (R1 on the diagram) between Jesus and the Father. Christ is presented to us as the Son living a life of union and communion with the Father in the Spirit, presenting himself in our humanity through the eternal Spirit to the Father on behalf of humankind. By his

Spirit he draws men and women to participate both in his life of worship and communion with the Father and in his mission from the Father to the world. "No one knows the Son except the Father and no one knows the Father except the Son and those to whom the Son chooses to reveal him" (Mt 11:27; Jn 1:18; 17:25-26). This unique relationship is described as one of mutual love, mutual self-giving, mutual testifying, mutual glorifying. Indeed there is a oneness of mind between the Father and the Son, revealed supremely in the cross, "to bring many sons to glory" (Heb 2:10), "that we might receive the adoption of sons" (Gal 4:5ff.)—that we might be drawn by the Spirit into that unique life of shared intimate communion. This is why Julian of Norwich could exclaim: "When I saw the Cross I saw the Trinity. . . . Where Jesus appears, the blessed Trinity is understood . . . The Trinity filled my heart full of the greatest joy, and I understood that it will be so in heaven without end."[5]

Likewise this unique relationship between Jesus and the Father is interpreted in terms of the Holy Spirit. Jesus is conceived by the Spirit, baptized by the Spirit, led by the Spirit into the wilderness. Through the eternal Spirit he offers himself to the Father on the cross and is raised from the dead by the Spirit. He receives the Spirit from the Father for us, vicariously, in his humanity, that out of his fullness he might baptize the church by the Spirit at Pentecost into a life of shared communion, mission, and service (R2 in the diagram).

A *twofold relationship* is thus established between the triune God and ourselves, through the Spirit. It is a relationship between God and humanity realized vicariously for us in Christ (R1), and at the same time a relationship between Christ and the church (R2), that we might participate by the Spirit in Jesus' communion with the Father in a life of intimate communion. In both, there is a bond of mutual love and mutual self-giving—of mutual "indwelling" (*perichōrēsis*, to use the word of the ancient church), of "perichoretic unity."

In virtue of this we can say with the apostle (1 Jn 1:13): "Truly our fellowship (*koinōnia*) is with the Father and with his Son Jesus Christ." The early Fathers expressed this by saying that he who was the eternal Son of God by nature became Son of Man, our brother, that we "sons (children) of men" might become "sons (children) of God" by grace—in him and through union with him. Thus, whether we are Jews or Gentiles, "through Christ, we both have access by one Spirit to the Father" (Eph 2:18).

The patristic phrase "one in being (*homoousios*) with the Father," betokens here that communion with Jesus Christ is communion with God. Therefore, to participate by the Spirit in the incarnate Christ's communion with the Father is to participate in the eternal Son's communion—a relationship which is both *internal* to the Godhead and *externally* extended to us by grace, established between God and humanity in the incarnation. The prime purpose of the incarnation, in the love of God, is to lift us up into a life of communion, of participation in the very triune life of God. Conversely, using Henry Scougal's phrase, in our communion with God we experience "the life of God in the soul of man."

In this understanding of worship we can discern a double movement of grace—(a) a God-humanward movement, from (*ek*) the Father, through (*dia*) the Son, in (*en*) the Spirit, and (b) a human-Godward movement to the Father, through the Son in the Spirit. This double movement of grace, which is the heart of the "dialogue" between God and humanity in worship, is grounded in the very perichoretic being of God, and is fundamental for our understanding of the triune God's relationship with the world in creation, incarnation and sanctification. What God is toward us in these relationships, he is in his innermost being.[6]

As we have seen, if the Father-Son relationship is not unique to Christ, but *generic* (as in the Harnack model where we are all sons and daughters of God), then all the great doctrines of our faith, the Trinity, incarnation, atonement, union with Christ, sacraments, etc. disappear. But conversely, if the Father-Son relationship given to us in Christ is *unique and absolute*, then the very opposite happens. The Trinity, the incarnation, once-and-for-all atonement, the one mediator, union with Christ, church as body of Christ, baptism and the Lord's Supper all unfold, as the Nicene Fathers saw. Furthermore, each of these doctrines must be interpreted in trinitarian terms, as for example we see in Von Balthasar's *Credo*—his exposition of the Apostles' Creed.

I think we can see that these three models represent different kinds of churchmanship in most of our churches. Probably the experience model is the most widespread.

A few years ago when lecturing in California, I was asked by a student, "What is wrong with that model? That is me! I was converted two years ago and gave my life to Christ." I replied that, as I saw it, there was nothing wrong in it as a description of genuine evangelical experience. From New Testament times onward, whenever the cross of Christ has been faithfully preached by Paul, John Stott or Billy Graham, people have come to faith and conversion. But do not build your theology on it! For then so much can go wrong. For example, what happens to our understanding of the Lord's Supper in that model? It reduces it to being merely a memorial of the death of Christ. Luther, Calvin and Knox all vigorously rejected such an interpretation. Baptism then becomes an outward sign of my faith, my decision, my conversion, my dying and rising (my subjective sanctification). But it is not my faith or my decision and conversion, my dying and rising which washes away my sins. It is Christ's vicarious baptism for us in blood on the cross, his death in which we, by grace, participate through water and the Spirit. Also the church, in this model, becomes simply the gathering of true believers with a common experience and less than a royal priesthood sharing in Christ's priesthood.

After one of my lectures in Seattle, an American Pentecostal minister, reflecting on the weakness of this model, said to me that for ten years he had been "whipping up" himself and his congregation to live out of their experience. He said: "I am weary and tired and have come to see that the center is all wrong. We feed upon Christ, the Bread of Life, not our own subjective experience." He resigned his ministry and came to Aberdeen to take a Ph.D., examining the trinitarian Christ-centered nature of authentic spirituality in the great saints of the church down through the ages. He described this discovery as his "conversion." More important than our experience of Christ is the Christ of our experience.

Our trinitarian model, as I see it, is a more authentic way of understanding genuine evangelical experience—experience grounded objectively in Jesus Christ, as in the evangelical hymns of Charles Wesley and Isaac Watts. In faith we look primarily away from ourselves to Jesus Christ, desiring to be found "in him," clothed with his righteousness (Phil 3:7-11).

In a remarkable way, much theology in the twentieth century has moved from model 1, through model 2, to model 3, to rediscover the centrality of the doctrines of the Trinity and the incarnation. Beginning with Adolf Harnack's 1900 lectures—a unitarian quest for the historical Jesus—it has moved through the "dialectical theology" or "theology of crisis" of the 1920s under the influence of Kierkegaardian insights and triggered by

Karl Barth's early *Romans* (1919), to Barth's concern in his *Church Dogmatics* (from 1932) to ground theology on the Trinity and the incarnation, followed in different ways by Rahner and Von Balthasar in Roman Catholic theology, and by Moltmann, Jüngel, T. F. Torrance, Colin Gunton, John Zizioulas and many others.

In November 1983, the British Council of Churches (B.C.C.), representing all the main denominations in this country, set up a Study Commission on Trinitarian Doctrine Today, which met for five years. They came to the unanimous conclusion that we all need to recover the centrality of the doctrine of the Trinity, and published three excellent booklets, each under the title of *The Forgotten Trinity*: (a) a report designed to be read by intelligent lay people, (b) a Bible study guide to be used in church study groups, and (c) a selection of papers on central trinitarian issues presented to the Commission.[7]

Why did the B.C.C. Commission feel so strongly that we must return to the great Christian doctrine of the Trinity? There were three main reasons:

1. We require a better doctrine of God. For too long, our concepts of God have been dominated by Plato, Aristotle, Stoic concepts of God as primarily the giver of natural law, the contract-God of Western jurisprudence who needs to be conditioned into being gracious by law being satisfied, static concepts of "substance," of God as an unmoved mover and an impassible first cause, etc. We need to recover a biblical understanding of God as the covenant God of grace, not a contract-God,[8] the God who has his loving Being-in-communion, and who has, in the freedom of his love, created us and redeemed us that we might find our true being in communion with him and one another.

2. We need to recover the doctrine of the Trinity for a better

understanding of worship—that all worship is the gift of participating through the Spirit in the incarnate Son's communion
with the Father, a gift of grace. Christian worship is trinitarian
in three main ways:

□ We pray to the Father, through the Son, in the Spirit. In all
the most ancient liturgies, prayer is primarily directed to God
as Father—as in the Lord's Prayer.

□ We pray to each of the three persons. We pray to the Father
and to the Son ("even so come, Lord Jesus") and to the Holy
Spirit (*Veni Creator Spiritus*) "who with the Father and the Son
together is worshiped and glorified" (Nicene Creed). Here we
see the significance of the Nicene "one in being" (*homoousios*).
We only pray to one God, but we have a warrant in the New
Testament and in the church's worship life to pray to each of
the three persons. Only one who has "the being of God" (*ousia*
of God) is creator, judge, redeemer, object of worship. The
Nicene Fathers saw in the light of the New Testament, in their
own experience in worship and in their debates with the Arians
and semi-Arians, that these can be predicated to each of the
three persons. Each has the *ousia* of God as creator, judge,
redeemer, object of worship. Hence they coined the word
homoousios, "one in being." Father, Son and Holy Spirit are
three in their distinctiveness, but "one in being."

□ We glorify the one God, Father, Son and Holy Spirit as when
we sing the doxology at the end of the Psalms.

But fundamental to all three trinitarian forms of worship is
the recognition that worship is the gift of grace. The Father has
given to us the Son and the Spirit to draw us into a life of shared
communion—of participating through the Spirit in the Son's
communion with the Father—that we might be drawn in love
into the very trinitarian life of God himself.

3. The B.C.C. Commission stressed that we need to recover

the doctrine of the Trinity for a better Christian anthropology—for a better understanding of the human person and community.

The Trinity and the Human Person

From the history of Christian thought, we can see that our doctrine of God reflects our understanding of humanity and, conversely, our understanding of the human being reflects our view of God. The counterpart of the rugged individualism of Western culture is the concept of a sovereign individual Monad "out there." The counterpart of the Protestant work ethic, as of much medieval Catholic piety, is the contract-God who rewards merit. The counterpart of Western concepts of the human person as an individual endowed with reason is a Stoic concept of God as the giver of natural law—engraved on the heart of the individual and discerned by the light of reason. The definition of Boethius (c. A.D. 480-525) which so influenced Western theology, *persona est individua substantia rationabilis naturae*, is historically a static concept of the individual as a substance possessing three faculties (reason, will and emotion), with primacy given to reason, which is identical in all individuals, governed by laws of non-contradiction and applied to all disciplines (be it the natural sciences, metaphysics or theology). Each individual has equal rights. Throughout, the dominating concept of God is, in practice at least, a unitarian one. God's primary purpose for humanity is legal, rational, individualistic. This concept of God and natural law—with the notions of "social contract," "contract of government," "contract of society"—was enormously influential in the rise of modern democracy.[9] The counterpart of the Christian doctrine of the Trinity, the God who has his being in loving communion, is clearly very different. His primary purpose for humanity is filial,

not just judicial—we have been created by God to find our true
being-in-communion, in sonship, in the mutual personal relationships of love. Here reason is understood, not statically or
substantively, but dynamically and functionally, as the capacity
of the whole person to respond to the other, of being true to
the truth, of "being true to one another in love" (*alētheuontes
en agapē:* Eph 4:15).[10]

What is needed today is a better understanding of the person
not just as an individual but as someone who finds his or her
true being in communion with God and with others, the
counterpart of a trinitarian doctrine of God. The God of the
New Testament is the God who has his true being as the Father
of the Son, and as the Son of the Father in the Spirit. God is
love and has his true being in communion, in the mutual
indwelling of Father, Son and Holy Spirit—*perichōrēsis*, the
patristic word. This is the God who has created us male and
female in his image to find our true humanity in perichoretic
unity with him and one another, and who renews us in his image
in Christ. Jesus said: "As the Father has loved me, so have I
loved you, so ought you to love one another" (Jn 15:9-13).

There is established for us in the gospel a threefold relation
of communion, mutual indwelling, perichoretic unity: (a) between Jesus and the Father in the Spirit, into which we are
drawn to participate (R1 in figure 3), (b) between Christ and
his body in the communion of the Spirit (as in the Eucharist)
(R2) and (c) between the members of the body by life in the
Spirit (as in marriage, Eph 5:25-33) (R3). This is what Karl
Barth has called "the analogy of relation," on which he sought
to ground a theological anthropology of co-humanity (*Mit-
menschlichkeit*) on the Trinity. As God has loved us and accepted
us freely and unconditionally in Christ, so we must love and
accept one another freely and unconditionally in him.

As in worship, so also in our personal relationships with one another, we are given the gift of participating through the Spirit in the incarnate Son's communion with the Father, in the trinitarian life of God. This means that perhaps we are never more truly human than at the Lord's Table, when Christ draws us into his life of communion with the Father and into communion with one another. God's purpose in Christ is "to create in himself a single new humanity" (Eph 2:15) to fulfill the purposes of creation and establish his kingdom.

In our modern world, in the tradition of Boethius and the Enlightenment, we usually equate the concept of "the person" with that of "the individual." But in a Christian understanding this is a mistake. Just as the words "father," "mother," "husband," "wife," "brother," "sister" are relational terms, so with the word "person." The human person is someone who finds his or her true being in relation, in love, in communion. For too long, Western theology has been dominated by a substance ontology of individuals with attributes in our interpretation of God, Jesus and ourselves as human beings. We need to recover, in the manner of the great Greek Fathers, Athanasius and the Cappadocian divines, a relational ontology to have a better doctrine of God and human personhood. John Zizioulas has argued strongly for this in his *Being as Communion*.[11]

This is a matter of great urgency in our culture where we witness, for example, the breakup of so many marriages. We have too one-sidedly interpreted the individual as someone with rights, duties (Thomas Jefferson), as the thinking self (Descartes), as endowed with reason (Boethius), as a self-legislating autonomous ego (Kant), as motivated by a work ethic, as someone with physical, economic, social, emotional, sexual and cultural needs. Two such individuals can legally contract together in marriage, but soon find their marriage on the rocks, as they claim individual rights to realize their own potential or see the other as simply there to meet their own needs. The relationship disintegrates because there is no real covenant love, no mutual self-giving and receiving, no perichoretic unity, no deep intimate communion.

Corresponding to this distinction between "the individual" and "the person," Professor John Macmurray, my moral philosophy teacher in undergraduate days in Edinburgh, used to draw a distinction between "society" and "community." He defined society as a collection of individuals indirectly related to one another by law, by employment, by contract, to meet needs (economic, financial, physical, etc.). Community, on the other hand, he defined as a group of persons in relation, directly related by love. He used to say that the fallacy of both Marxism and much of capitalism is the pragmatic naive belief that if we can simply change the economic structures of society, we can produce community. "You don't!" he said, "You can destroy it." After 70 years of communism, Eastern Europe has thrown off its yoke, for the people have seen its failure to produce a free community, a classless society. We can see a similar result in forms of Western capitalism, which attempts to subordinate, everything to market forces. It can produce massive unemployment, polarize rich and poor, undermine health services and fail to show compassion in contexts where there comes the cry for justice and humanity from the poor and powerless. The concept of community, Macmurray contended, is a religious notion, deriving from a Hebrew Christian consciousness. From a trinitarian standpoint, God is in the business of creating community. We are, of course, social beings who live in society with our economic, financial and political needs, but a compassionate government should seek to make a loving, caring community possible.

It is significant that the older individualism grew out of a belief in the objectivity of God—the Creator of natural and moral law, who created the individual, with rights to life, liberty and the pursuit of happiness (the American Constitution). But what happens in a secular culture where belief in the objectivity of God and of moral law recedes? Then, as Allan Bloom has argued so powerfully in *The Closing of the American Mind*,[12] everything goes into flux (Heraclitus), and we witness a closing of the (American) mind, with a resultant collapse into narcissism, a preoccupation with the self—my rights, my life, my liberty, my pursuit of happiness. Religion then becomes a means toward self-realization. All the interest is in self-esteem, self-fulfillment, self-identity, the human potential movement and possibility thinking, leading either to the nihilism of post-modernism[13] or to the neo-gnosticism of the New Age movement which identifies the self with God. Know yourself. Realize your own identity. Then you will know God in the depths of your own spirituality. Hence the cry for new images of God to express our own self-understanding and sexuality. We shall return to this later.

What is the Christian answer? Is it to go back to Plato's *Republic*, as Allan Bloom suggests, to recover the objectivity of truth, beauty, goodness, justice? Is it to revive the older notions of natural law and moral law discerned by the kindly light of reason, with their concomitant individualism? Or is it not rather to return to "the forgotten Trinity"—to an understanding of the Holy Spirit, who delivers us from a narcissistic preoccupation with the self to find our true being in loving communion with God and one another—to hear God's call to us, in our day, to participate through the Spirit in Christ's communion with the Father and his mission from the Father to the world—to create in our day a new humanity of persons who find true fulfillment in other-centered communion and service in the kingdom of God?

Chapter Two

The Sole Priesthood of Christ, the Mediator of Worship

WHILE LECTURING ON THE THEOLOGY OF WORSHIP for Fuller Theological Seminary in California, I was living in an apartment on the Balboa Peninsula, 200 yards from the sea. One day, as I was about to have a swim, I saw an elderly gentleman walking slowly, pensively, along the shore. I greeted him as I went into the sea. When I came out, he was just returning and came to ask me who I was and where I had come from. I told him I was from Scotland, a Presbyterian minister on a lecturing-preaching tour of the States. His face lit up and he said, "How astonishing that I should meet you just now!" Then he poured out his story.

After 45 years of happy married life, his wife was now dying of cancer. She had had serious surgery. "I've been walking up and down the streets of Newport Beach at night, desperate, because I do not know how to face the future without my wife—and without faith," he added. Then he said, "My father was a Presbyterian minister, and I was brought up in a godly home. But I have drifted away from the church. When you spoke to me, I was remembering how my father was a man of prayer and had wonderful faith when my mother died. I wish I had that faith. I have been walking up and down this beach trying to pray, but I can't!"

What did I say to him? Did I tell him how to find faith and how to pray—throw him back on himself? No I did not. I said, "May I say to you what I am sure your father would have said to you? In Jesus Christ we have someone who knows all about this. He has been through it all—through suffering and death and separation—and he will carry you both through it into resurrection life. He has heard your cry for faith and is answering." I continued, "You have been walking up and down this beach, wanting to pray, trying to pray, but not knowing how to pray. In Jesus Christ we have someone who is praying for you. He has heard your groans and is interceding for you and with you and in you." Then I took him to Luke 22:31, where Jesus says to Peter in the hour of his temptation (see also v. 40), "Simon, Simon, Satan has desired to sift you as wheat. But I have prayed for you, Simon, that your faith may not fail . . ." In spite of this, Peter denied his Lord. Jesus was taken away to be crucified. But the risen Lord came back to him and said, "Simon, do you love me?" Peter said, "Lord, you know I love you" (Jn 21:15ff.). He was upheld, even in his denial of Christ, by the intercessions of Christ. I also took my friend to some verses in Romans 8:26ff., where Paul says, "The Spirit helps us in our weakness. We do not know how to pray as we ought, but the Spirit himself intercedes for us with groans that words cannot express." I said, "None of us knows how to pray, but the Spirit knows all about us. He knows all about you and is interpreting your desires and groans and your longing to know how to pray. He is interceding for you and leading you to the Father." Then I quoted the following verses in that chapter: "Who is he who condemns? Christ Jesus who died—more than that, who was raised to life—is at the right hand of God and is also interceding for us"—therefore "nothing shall separate us from the love of God"—not even death! I prayed with him there on the beach.

The next day he came looking for me and said, "I have been telling my wife what you told me! Tell me more!" The third day he came again: "Do me a favor! Come and speak to my wife!" "Of course," I said. He took me to her bedside. There she was, a frail, dying woman. What did I talk to them about? I spoke about the Trinity! I did not use that word. But I spoke to them about the loving God, our Father who has given us Christ and the Spirit to draw us to himself in prayer, and about Jesus Christ who died for us that we might be forgiven, receive the gift of sonship, and be led by the Spirit into eternal life. I spoke about Christ, our great high priest, touched with a feeling of our infirmities, interceding for us, opening our hearts by the Spirit. I prayed with them both. A few weeks later, he wrote to me to tell me that his wife had passed on—"safe in the arms of Jesus."

It seems to me that in a pastoral situation our first task is not to throw people back on themselves with exhortations and instructions as to what to do and how to do it, but to direct people to the gospel of grace—to Jesus Christ, that they might look to him to lead them, open their hearts in faith and in prayer, and draw them by the Spirit into his eternal life of communion with the Father. The Christian doctrine of the Trinity is the grammar of Romans 8—the grammar of grace, the grammar of our pastoral work. The first real step on the road to prayer is to recognize that none of us knows how to pray as we ought to. But as we bring our desires to God, we find that we have someone who is praying for us, with us, and in us. Thereby he teaches us to pray and motivates us to pray, and to pray in peace to the Lord. Jesus takes our prayers—our feeble, selfish, inarticulate prayers—he cleanses them, makes them his prayers, and in a "wonderful exchange" (*mirifica commutatio—commercium admirabile*)[1] he makes his prayers our prayers and presents us to the Father as his dear children, crying: "*Abba* Father."

The Interceding Christ

For a proper understanding of prayer we need to recover the New Testament teaching about the sole priesthood of Christ—that we have someone who stands in for us to do for us and in us what we try to do and fail to do—someone who lives forever to intercede for us (Heb 6:20; 7:25-28; 8:1-6) and who gives us the gift of the Spirit to share in his intercessions.

In the Westminster Shorter Catechism, which many of us were taught as children in Scotland, there is a statement on prayer:

Q. What is prayer?

A. Prayer is an offering up of our desires unto God for things agreeable to his will, *in the name of Christ*, with confession of our sins and thankful acknowledgment of his mercies.

We can only pray "in the name of Christ" because Christ has already, in our name, offered up our desires to God and continues to offer them. In our name, he lived a life agreeable to the will of God, in our name vicariously confessed our sins and submitted to the verdict of guilty for us, and in our name gave thanks to God. We pray "in the name of Christ" because of what Christ has done and is doing today in our name, on our behalf.

This finds vivid expression in what the New Testament says about the priesthood of Christ in his ministry of prayer and intercession—as in our Lord's high priestly prayer in John 17, and in the epistle to the Hebrews, which uses the liturgical symbolism of the worship of Old Testament Israel to interpret the ministry of Christ.

In Old Testament Israel, as in Israel to this day, the great central act of Jewish worship took place on the Day of Atonement (*yôm kippúr*). That was the day in the year which gathered up the worship of every other day. On that day, an offering was made to God which gathered up all the other offerings made daily in the sanctuary. On that day, the worship and intercessions of all Israel were led by one man, the high priest.

Consider for a moment the symbolism of that day. First, the high priest stood before the people as their divinely appointed representative, bone of their bone, flesh of their flesh, their brother, in solidarity with the people he represented, "the one on behalf of the many," the "leader of their worship."[2] All that he did, he did in their name. This was symbolized by the fact that he bore their names engraved on his breastplate and shoulders as a memorial before God. Secondly, he consecrated himself for this ministry by certain liturgical acts of washing and sacrifice, the blood sprinkled on his right ear, right thumb and right toe. Thirdly, there comes the great moment when he takes an animal, lays his hands on the victim and vicariously confesses the sins of all Israel in an act of penitence, acknowledging the just judgments of God. Fourthly, when the victim is immolated as a symbol of the just judgments of God (and the scapegoat is sent into the wilderness to symbolize the removal of guilt) the high priest takes the blood in a vessel, ascends into the Holy of Holies, and there vicariously intercedes for all Israel—that God will remember his covenant promises and graciously forgive

them. We can visualize the high priest in the sanctuary interceding for all Israel, and all Israel outside interceding—a great
volume of prayer ascending to God, led by the high priest.
Finally, he returns to the waiting people outside with the
Aaronic blessing of peace:

> The LORD bless you
>   and keep you;
> the LORD make his face shine upon you
>   and be gracious to you;
> the LORD turn his face toward you
>   and give you peace. (Num 6:24-26 NIV)

The New Testament writers saw this as a foreshadowing of the
mediatorial ministry of Christ. Firstly, he comes from the Father
to be the true priest, bone of our bone, flesh of our flesh, in
solidarity with all humanity, all races, all colors, bearing upon
his divine-human heart the names, the needs, the sorrows, the
injustices of all nations. He offers to the Father that worship,
that obedience, that life of love in unbroken intimate communion, which we cannot offer. Secondly, he consecrates himself
for this ministry of leading us into the presence of the Father.
In our Lord's high priestly prayer, when he intercedes for his
people, he says: "For their sakes I sanctify myself that they also
might be sanctified through the truth" (Jn 17:19)—the one for
the many—"For both he who sanctifies and they who are
sanctified are all of one, for . . . he is not ashamed to call them
brothers (and sisters)" (Heb 2:11). Jesus' whole life of prayer
and obedience and love, his whole life of communion in the
Spirit, is his total self-consecration for us. Thirdly, he offers not
an animal, but himself in death that he might be the Lamb of
God to take away the sin of the world, saying amen in our
humanity to the just judgments of God. He does not appease
an angry God to condition him into being gracious, but in

perfect acknowledgment of the holy love of the Father for a sinful world, seals God's covenant purposes for all humanity by his blood. Fourthly, on Easter day he says to Mary, "Do not hold on to me for I am not yet ascended to my Father, but go instead to my brothers and say to them, I ascend to my Father and your Father, to my God and your God" (Jn 20:17). The high priest is on his way into the Holy of Holies to intercede for his people. Fifthly, on the same day at evening, as the disciples are met in prayer in an upper room, Jesus comes and says to them, "Peace be unto you" (v. 19ff.). It is the return of the high priest who now gives the gift of the Spirit that they might share with him his apostolic mission to the world (see also Heb 3:1) as a royal priesthood with the word of forgiveness.

When we think of the symbolism of the liturgy of Old Testament Israel on the Day of Atonement, we can make two statements, enshrining the biblical concept of "the one and the many":

□ When the high priest entered into the holy presence of Yahweh in the sanctuary, that he might present all Israel in his person to God, we can say, as Calvin puts it in his commentary on Hebrews,[3] all Israel entered in his person.

□ Conversely, when he vicariously confessed their sins and interceded for them before God, God accepted them as his forgiven people in the person of their high priest.

This double statement expresses how God's covenant dealings with Israel were established at the hands of a mediator.

In analogous fashion, we can make a twofold statement about Jesus Christ, in the light of the New Testament:

□ When Jesus was born for us at Bethlehem, was baptized by the Spirit in the Jordan, suffered under Pontius Pilate, rose again and ascended, our humanity was born again, baptized by the Spirit, suffered, died, rose again and ascended in him, in his representative vicarious humanity. Now he presents us in himself to the Father as God's dear children, and our righteousness is hid with Christ in God—ready to be revealed at the last day. □ Conversely, because Jesus has lived our life, offered himself through the eternal Spirit without spot to the Father in our name and on our behalf, as the one for the many, God accepts us in him. We are accepted in the beloved Son—immaculate in him, and only in him—"holy and blameless in his sight" (*sancti et immaculati*) (Eph 1:4).[4]

This is the significance when we pray "in the name of Christ." Because of what he has done and is doing for us in our name, we worship the Father *in Christ* as well as *through Christ, en Christō* as well as *dia Christou*. As Calvin said also of justification, we are righteous *in Christ*, as well as justified by faith *through* the work of *Christ*.[5] Jesus is the Mediator of the new covenant, the one in whom God draws near to humanity in covenant love and the one in whom we draw near to God through the Spirit. In worship we offer ourselves to the Father "in the name of Christ" because he has already in our name made the one true offering to the Father, the offering by which he has sanctified for all time those who come to God by him (Heb 10:10, 14), and because he ever lives to intercede for us in our name. The covenant between God and humanity is concentrated in his person.

The One and the Many

This biblical thought of "the one and the many," of the all-inclusive humanity of Jesus Christ, must be carefully distinguished from the Platonic (or Hindu) concept of "the one and the many." In so-called Platonic realism "the one" is an idea, a generic class concept, a Platonic form, where the important thing is "the one," not the many particulars which are what they are only in virtue of their participation (*methexis*) in "the one." Knowledge for Plato consists of ideas, the universal, the class concept, not of the particular, not of sense objects as such. Particulars, sense data, belong to the world of flux and change and temporality—here today, gone tomorrow (Heraclitus)—not, therefore, objects of knowledge. Universals are timeless, unchanging, abstract concepts (Parmenides)—the objects of knowledge.

For example, if I see a yellow flower on a bank in spring and ask, What is it? and the answer is a primrose, I know what it is by subsuming it under the class of primroses. My interest is in what it is, not so much in the particular instance as a sense object. But the biblical notion of "the one and the many," the thought of the all-inclusive humanity of Christ, is totally different, where the many participate (*koinōnein*) personally in the one. It is not just a Platonic concept of Jesus as an ideal embodiment of humanity. If it were, then the important thing would be not Jesus as an absolutely unique particular person, but the ideal, the principle he embodied. The New Testament is thoroughly non-dualistic about Jesus being not only a man, but the One Man, the one person in whom God has given himself personally to the world and for the world, that his purposes for all humanity might be brought to fulfillment. There is an absolute uniqueness to the person of Jesus Christ, deeply concerned for every single one of the many to bring every single one into personal union with himself, to share his personal union with the Father. Thus in Jesus Christ "the one and the many" means at once the one for the many, the one who stands in for the many, the many represented personally in the one, the one who comes by the Spirit to each one of the many whom he loves and knows by name to say: "It is for you,

John, and for you, Mary, and for you, Peter." Whereas the Platonic "one and the many" is impersonal and disinterested in the particular, the biblical "one and the many" is intensely personal.

It is this thought of an all-inclusive vicarious humanity which was developed by Irenaeus in his doctrine of *anakephalaiōsis* or recapitulation. Like Justin Martyr before him, he attacked Marcion's attempt to distinguish between the creator God of the Old Testament and the redeemer God of the New Testament. The Christ by whom all things were made is the same Christ who, for us and our salvation, assumed our humanity. In other words, the Son of God who created Adam for sonship and communion and immortality does not abandon his loving purposes for humanity, for every single human person. But in order to redeem humanity and to bring to fulfillment his purpose (his *telos*) for humanity, for everyone, he himself becomes a man that he might fulfill for us in his own person God's purposes of love and obedience and worship. Thus what is lost in the one man ("in Adam")—communion with God—is restored and fulfilled for each one of us in Christ ("the last Adam"), and held out for us by the Spirit in the Lord's Supper. This, of course, is the Pauline doctrine of Romans 5 and Ephesians 1—that God's great purpose is that "he might gather together in one all things in Christ" (Eph 1:10).

This concept of recapitulation, of the fulfillment of God's purposes for humanity in and through the inclusive and vicarious humanity of Christ, received fuller elaboration by Athanasius, Cyril of Alexandria, and the Cappadocian divines in their statement that "the unassumed is the unredeemed" in reply to Apollinarianism.[6] The Greek Fathers, like Athanasius, asked what it means to speak of Christ as "the great physician of our humanity." Christ does not heal us as an ordinary doctor might, by standing over against us, diagnosing our sickness, prescribing medicine for us to take and then going away, leaving us to get better as we follow his instructions. No, he becomes the patient! He assumes that very humanity which is in need of redemption, and by being anointed by the Spirit in our humanity, by a life of perfect obedience, by dying and rising again, for us, our humanity is healed in him, in his person. We are not just healed through Christ, because of the work of Christ, but in and through Christ. Person and work must not be separated. That is why these Fathers did not hesitate to say, as Edward Irving, the Scottish theologian in the early nineteenth century and Karl Barth in our own times have said, that Christ assumed "fallen humanity" (i.e., our humanity) that it might be turned back to God, in him by his sinless life in the Spirit, and through him in us.

The God-humanward and human-Godward relationship (movement), both freely given to us in Jesus Christ. When we considered the existential model of worship, we noticed that the God-humanward movement of grace is given to us in Christ. In virtue of it, we are summoned to respond in faith, in decision, in repentance and obedience (see figure 2). But the weakness here is that the only human-Godward movement is ours. In other words, it does not do full justice to the meaning of grace, for it short-circuits the vicarious humanity of Christ. Grace does not only mean that in the coming of Jesus Christ, God gives himself in holy love to humanity. It also means the coming of God as man, to do for us as a man what we cannot do for ourselves—to present us in himself through the eternal Spirit to the Father. In other words, the human-Godward movement, in which we are given to participate (as in worship and communion), is given freely and unconditionally. Our response in faith and obedience is a response to the response

already made for us by Christ to the Father's holy love, a
response we are summoned to make in union with Christ. This,
it seems to me, was the great insight of the Greek fathers like
Cyril of Alexandria, elaborated by John Calvin in his *Institutes*.
He expounded grace in terms of the twin doctrines that "all
parts of our salvation are already complete in Christ" in virtue
of his obedience for us, and that we are summoned to a life of
"union with Christ" to become in ourselves what we already
are in Christ our head.[7]

Few distinctions in theology are more important for our
understanding of worship than that discussed by Calvin in book
3 of the *Institutes*, between what he calls "legal repentance" and
"evangelical repentance" in his critique of the medieval sacrament
of penance.[8] Legal repentance says: "Repent, and if you repent
you will be forgiven!" as though God our Father has to be
conditioned into being gracious. It makes the imperatives of
obedience prior to the indicatives of grace, and regards God's love
and forgiveness and acceptance as conditional upon what we
do—upon our meritorious acts of repentance. Calvin argued that
this inverted the evangelical order of grace, and made repentance
prior to forgiveness, whereas in the New Testament forgiveness is
logically prior to repentance. Evangelical repentance, on the other
hand, takes the form: "Christ has borne your sins on the cross;
therefore, repent! Receive his forgiveness in repentance!" That is,
repentance is our response to grace, not a condition of grace. The
goodness of God leads us to repentance. The good news of the
gospel is that "there is forgiveness with God that he might be
feared," and that he has spoken that word of forgiveness in Christ
on the cross. That word summons from us an unconditional
response of faith and repentance.

What did Calvin mean by saying that forgiveness is logically
prior to repentance? The point is of fundamental importance

in our personal relationships. If two people have the misfortune to quarrel, and one comes to the other and says, in all sincerity, "I forgive you!" it is clearly not only a word of love and reconciliation, but also a word (perhaps a withering word) of condemnation—for in pronouncing his forgiveness, he is clearly implying that the other is the guilty party! Indeed it can be very hurtful, if not self-righteous, to say to somebody, "I forgive you!" How would the other person be likely to react? I could imagine his immediate reaction as one of indignation. Sensing the element of judgment, of condemnation in the word, he might well reject the forgiveness, because he refuses to submit to the verdict of guilty implied in it. He would be impenitent. There would be no change of heart. But, suppose on subsequent reflection he comes back to his friend and says, "You were quite right! I was in the wrong!" Implicit in his acceptance of love and forgiveness would be his submission to the verdict of guilty. There would be a real change of mind, an act of penitence on his part (*metanoia*), conversion, reconciliation.

So it is with the gospel of the incarnation. God in Christ has spoken to us his word of forgiveness, his word of love which is at the same time the word of judgment and condemnation, the word of the cross. But implicit in our receiving of the word of grace and forgiveness, the word of the Father's love, there must be on our part, a humble submission to the verdict of guilty. It was for our sins that Christ died. That lies at the heart of the Reformation understanding of grace—of "evangelical repentance." But who can make that perfect response of love, that perfect act of penitence, that perfect submission to the verdict of guilty? What we cannot do, God has done for us in Jesus Christ. Jesus Christ stands in for us in our humanity, in our name, on our behalf, to make that perfect submission to the

Father. That is the wonder of God's grace! God not only speaks the word of forgiveness to us. He also provides for us one, in Jesus Christ, who makes the perfect response of vicarious penitence. So God accepts us, not because of our repentance—we have no worthy penitence to offer—but in the person of one who has already said amen for us, in death, to the divine condemnation of our sin—in atonement.[9]

Here again we see the significance of a biblical understanding of priesthood, and especially the significance of the priesthood of Christ, the mediator of worship. His twofold ministry of representing God to humanity and at the same time of representing humanity to God brings God's word of grace and forgiveness to the world, because he vicariously submitted for us, once and for all, to the divine judgment on our sins, accepting the verdict of guilty on the cross, not for himself, but for us. This was foreshadowed in the liturgy of the Old Testament. On the Day of Atonement, the high priest, in representing Yahweh to Israel and Israel to Yahweh, brought God's word of grace and acceptance to the people and, on behalf of all Israel, confessed their sins by bearing witness to God's judgment in offering the sacrificial victim and sprinkling the blood on the propitiatory. So in Jesus Christ we have one who, as the Word incarnate, brings the Father's word of grace and forgiveness to our fallen world, but who in our fallen humanity vicariously absorbs the Father's condemnation of our sins—being made a curse for us. Therefore, in our response, in our worship, we not only in faith receive that word of forgiveness so freely spoken, but we receive it in repentance, submitting humbly to the guilty verdict (which is repentance) before the cross. At the same time we know that by God's grace we have one in Christ, who has already submitted to that verdict for us long ago. Our repentance is thus a response to grace, not a condition of grace. It is the gift of the Spirit to participate in the vicarious penitence of Christ, in his priestly vicarious self-offering. It is our amen to the cross, our response to the amen spoken by Jesus Christ standing in our place before the Father. It is "evangelical repentance." It is the meaning of conversion.

It is significant that the Roman Catholic church today prefers to talk about the sacrament of reconciliation rather than the sacrament of penance. Is this not a recognition of the fact that repentance is not a meritorious act which conditions God into being gracious (legal repentance), but rather our receiving the word of grace and reconciliation in an act of humble faith and penitence—what Calvin called "evangelical repentance"? God's grace is unconditionally free, but it summons us to receive it unconditionally in faith and penitence, in love and obedience.

The fact that Jesus Christ is the leader of our worship, the high priest who forgives us our sins and leads us into the holy presence of the Father, is the central theme of the epistle to the Hebrews. It was written to Christians who had at one time looked to Jesus Christ in faith and followed him, but then had taken their eyes off Christ and fallen back into their former religious practices, with a false legalistic self-confidence in human institutions and ordinances. The Christians who had led them to Christ, whose example they once followed, were now dead (13:7). Instead of going on to become leaders and teachers themselves (5:12), they had drifted away from Christ, lost their vision of grace, and now needed again to be taught the elementary principles of the faith (5:12-14). By their un-faithfulness, like Israel in the wilderness, they were unable to enter into the "rest" of the promised land. They were in danger of sinking into apostasy. So the writer seeks to give them a fresh vision of Jesus Christ, our high priest, through whom alone we can find forgiveness and come into the holy presence of God.

He exhorts them to fix their thoughts exclusively on Christ, to hold on in faith, not to drift away in unbelief or rely on their own religious practices to cleanse them. They had apparently suffered persecution and reproach, and by yielding to the temptation to be unfaithful, had drifted away from Christ. The writer reminds them that Christ himself had suffered (12:2) and been tempted. He could, therefore, sympathize with them and lead them in their time of trial and need (4:14-16; 5:1-5). "Let us run with patience the race set before us. Let us fix our eyes on Jesus, the author and perfecter of our faith, who for the joy set before him endured the cross, scorning the shame, and sat down at the right hand of God. Consider him who endured such opposition from sinful men, so that you will not grow weary and lose heart" (12:1-4).

The epistle, in calling these lapsed Christians back to Christ, clearly expounds the place of Jesus Christ in worship, contrasting it with the old Levitical rites to which the people had apparently returned. The apostle Paul in the epistle to the Romans speaks about "the righteous requirements" (*dikaiōmata*) of the (moral) law—to love God and our neighbor—having been fulfilled for us only by Christ and now fulfilled in us by a life in the Spirit (Rom 8:1-4). Similarly, the writer to the Hebrews speaks about "the `ordinances of worship" (*dikaiōmata latreias*, Heb 9:1) having been fulfilled for us only by Jesus Christ our high priest, so that we can draw near to God only through him. He alone can wash away our sins, who offered himself for us to God through the eternal Spirit. The apostle Paul contrasts life in the Spirit with a false confidence in the flesh (*sarx*). The writer to the Hebrews speaks about the other forms of worship, the external ritual of human gifts and sacrifices, food and drink etc., which can never cleanse the conscience, as the "requirements of the flesh" (*dikaiōmata sarkos*) (v. 10). In other words, as Paul expounds justification by faith by contrasting life in the Spirit—the way of grace—with false self-confidence in the flesh, so the epistle to the Hebrews contrasts two forms of worship: true worship, which means reposing on and participating in the self-offering of Christ who alone can lead us into "the Holy of Holies"—the holy presence of the Father—and false worship, with its false reliance on what we do by following our own devices or traditions. In other words, when we take our eyes off Jesus Christ and that worship and offering which God has provided for us in Christ, which alone is acceptable to him, we fall back on our "religion."

This seems to me to be relevant to the distinction we drew at the beginning of our study between the two views of worship—a unitarian view that worship is what we, religious people, do to try to please God, and a trinitarian one, where worship is the gift of grace to participate through the Spirit in the incarnate Son's communion with the Father—the way of joy and peace and confidence. The church which takes her eyes off Jesus Christ, the only mediator of worship, is on the road to becoming apostate. There is no more urgent need in our churches today than to recover the trinitarian nature of grace— that it is by grace alone, through the gift of Jesus Christ in the Spirit that we can enter into and live a life of communion with God our Father. We can understand why John Calvin made so much of the epistle to the Hebrews—of the doctrine of the once and for all, and continuing priesthood of Jesus Christ—in his exposition of worship, the Eucharist, and the doctrine of the church as a corporate royal priesthood participating by grace in the sole priesthood of Christ. This interpretation of worship and the church in terms of grace—of Christ as the sole mediator between God and humanity—is fundamental to the Reformed tradition and to our understanding of prayer (1 Tim 2:1-6).

According to a biblical understanding, from both the Old
and New Testaments, worship is an ordinance of grace. It is
false to interpret Old Testament worship as legalistic and only
New Testament worship as the way of grace. As we have seen,
there is always a double movement in worship—a God-humanward movement and a human-Godward movement—and both
must be understood in terms of the gift of grace, the gift of the
God of grace who provides for us a way of loving communion.
In Old Testament Israel, the priest who represented God to
Israel and Israel to God had a double function. Primarily, he
was the one who brought God's word of grace to Israel. This
was the word of the covenant with its promises and obligations:
"I will be your God and you will be my people." Secondarily,
he was the one who led the people in their worship, their
response to grace. The liturgies of Israel were God-given
ordinances of grace, witnesses to grace.[10] The sacrifice of lambs
and bulls and goats were not ways of placating an angry God,
currying favor with God as in the pagan worship of the Baalim.
They were God-given covenantal witnesses to grace—that the
God who alone could wipe out their sins would be gracious.
God is always the subject of propitiation, never its object. He
gave Israel forms of worship which testified to his holy love,
that he would be gracious and propitious, and in their worship
they were to acknowledge this. But so often the priests failed
to fulfill their primary task of being bearers of God's word of
grace. When this happened, their worship was no longer a
response to grace, but became a form of legalized liturgy, a way
of trying to manipulate God and curry favor—in the manner
of the Canaanite Baalim. When this happened, God raised up
prophets, many of them out of the priesthood, to bring God's
word of grace, the word of the covenant with its solemn
obligations, to the people of Israel. They exposed both the false

practices of the priests and the unrighteousness of the nation which had turned its back on the God of grace, on the covenant made with Abraham and renewed at Sinai. They exposed the paganism of the rituals and the legalism of their belief that their sacrifices were efficacious in themselves. So God can say to them, through Amos:

I hate, I despise your religious feasts;
I cannot stand your assemblies.
Even though you bring me burnt offerings and grain
offerings,
I will not accept them.
Though you bring choice peace offerings,
I will have no regard for them.
Away with the noise of your songs!
I will not listen to the music of your harps.
But let justice roll on like a river,
righteousness like a never-failing stream! (Amos 5:21-24)

In other words, where worship is no longer seen as an ordinance of and an obedient response to grace, it has become false worship—an abomination to God who says "Take it away!"

The same was true of the temple and its worship. When the temple was no longer a faithful witness to God's covenant purposes, and the priests failed to offer true worship, God permitted it to be destroyed, that he might, in the fullness of time establish true worship in the world—as in Ezekiel's visions of a new temple.

As with the temple so with the nation of Israel itself. Israel was elected from among the nations to be a "royal priesthood," a covenanted nation, living by God's grace, the servant of Yahweh, to be "a light to the Gentiles," to live as a righteous nation before God a life of undivided loyalty to him (Ex 19:4-8). But when Israel turned to worship in the manner of the pagan nations around them, God permitted them to be taken into exile, that he might make a new beginning with the faithful remnant who would return from exile. So there emerged the visions of the suffering servant of the Lord, through whom God would fulfill his purposes of grace and provide one who would take away their sins and renew them in righteousness. God acts in judgment and in mercy in the history of Israel that he might fashion a faithful people who would offer true worship to the God of grace.

The same pattern is repeated dramatically and vividly with Moses, Aaron, and the golden calf. Moses went up the mountain into the holy presence of God—the Holy of Holies—to commune with God and bring back to Israel the word of the covenant with its summons to a life of faithfulness and obedience. His brother Aaron, as high priest, might then lead Israel in her worship to fulfill the ordinances of grace in a faithful response in love and obedience. But what happened? We read: "When the people saw that Moses was so long in coming down from the mountain, they gathered round Aaron and said, 'Come, make us gods who will go before us. As for this fellow Moses who brought us up out of Egypt, we don't know what has happened to him' " (Ex 32:1). Aaron listened to the people and they made a golden calf as assertion of their own nature worship, a fertility cult expressive of their own self-will and desire to escape from the living God. Instead of their worship being an ordinance of grace and a covenanted way of response, it becomes a rebellious, idolatrous form of self-expression and self-assertion. As a result they expose themselves to divine judgment. Miriam is struck with leprosy, the glory leaves the holy place, and a heartbroken Moses intercedes for his unfaithful nation. The people remain in the desert to die, and only a faithful few enter the promised land—used as a warning in Hebrews 3:12ff.

It is significant that in Christian history, when the medieval Roman Catholic Church too often neglected her prime function of being a minister of grace—bringing the word of grace, of the new covenant in Christ—the character of worship changed. With notions of merit and penance and an efficacious mass, the church was seen as a "treasury of merit" (*thesaurus meritorum*) with a legalized liturgy, a church claiming "the power of the keys." In response the Reformation emerged as a prophetic movement, with many of the Reformers, like Luther, coming from the priesthood itself to call the church back to her foundations in grace, and to reinterpret her worship, as in the Lord's Supper, as an ordinance of grace, seeing sacraments as signs and seals of the covenant of grace.

The very unfaithfulness of Israel and her priesthood in their worship, in failing to be custodians of grace, thrust up the messianic hopes of a faithful servant of the Lord, fulfilled in Jesus Christ. Jesus Christ is, on the one hand, God's Word of grace to a faithless world, the one in whom God makes a new covenant, bringing forgiveness (Jer 31:31ff.). But on the other hand, he is the one whose whole vicarious life in our humanity is a faithful obedient response to the Father's purpose in electing him—in fulfilling the role of the suffering servant of the Lord, in being the Lamb of God to take away the sin of the world—that through him Israel's destiny to be a light to the Gentiles might be fulfilled. Here is the one true priest, the one true worshiper, the leader of our worship (the *leitourgos*) in whom alone "the ordinances of worship" (*dikaiōmata latreias*) are perfectly fulfilled and through whom alone we can draw near to God. So worship is God's gift of grace to us in Christ. This is why all our worship (in baptism, Lord's Supper, etc.) must be seen as an ordinance of grace.

J. Jungmann, the Jesuit liturgical scholar, in his great work *The Place of Christ in Liturgical Prayer*,[11] has shown that in the New Testament and the early liturgies of the church, Christ has a double role. On the one hand, prayer was offered to Jesus Christ as God. We pray to the Father and to the Son and to the Holy Spirit. But on the other hand, Jesus Christ was seen as our great high priest, as man praying to the Father, the one who intercedes for us and leads our praises and prayers. Then, at the time of the Arian-Nicene controversy, one of Arius's main arguments against the deity of Christ was that Jesus could not be God because he was a man who prayed to God—as in the gospel accounts of Jesus praying at his baptism, on the mountainside, at the Last Supper, in Gethsemane and on the cross. He cannot be both God and a man praying to God! Athanasius's reply was: "Arius, you do not understand the meaning of grace!"

The God to whom we pray and with whom we commune knows we want to pray, try to pray, but cannot pray. So God comes to us as man in Jesus Christ to stand in for us, pray for us, teach us to pray and lead our prayers. God in grace gives us what he seeks from us—a life of prayer—in giving us Jesus Christ and the Spirit. So Christ is very God, the God to whom we pray. And he is very man, the man who prays for us and with us. The Nicene Fathers, with their study of the place of Jesus Christ in worship, won the day—and so we have the Nicene Creed. But, Jungmann points out, fear of Arianism and the Arian argument—pitting the praying humanity of Jesus against the deity of Christ—led the church, while asserting powerfully the deity of Christ, to play down the priesthood of Christ! What was the result? The church, the *ecclesia*, took over the vicarious role of being the high priest for humanity! While strongly asserting the divinity of Christ and his kingly, prophetic role, the church assumed the role of being the mediator of grace, with the added vicarious roles of Mary and the saints. We can, therefore, understand the emphasis of Reformers like John Calvin. He called the church back to the sole priesthood of Christ as both the object of our worship and the leader of our worship. He reinterpreted the church as the royal priesthood that shares by grace in the priesthood of Christ. Only in this way can we understand our Christian worship as an ordinance of grace, where Christ is the only mediator. We come to God our Father both in Christ and through Christ, and only through Jesus Christ.

It is supremely in Jesus Christ that we see the double meaning of grace. Grace means that God gives himself to us as God, freely and unconditionally, to be worshiped and adored. But grace also means that God comes to us in Jesus Christ as man, to do for us and in us what we cannot do. He offers a life of perfect obedience and worship and prayer to the Father, that we might be drawn by the Spirit into communion with the Father, "through Jesus Christ our Lord."

The two hands of God. A colleague of mine for many years, Roland Walls, lives in the Community of the Transfiguration in Roslin village, a few miles out of Edinburgh. One day I noticed in his garden a piece of sculpture I had not seen before. He told me about it. A young sculptor, brought up among the Exclusive Brethren, one day confessed to the fellowship that he was gay. As a result, he was asked to leave the Assembly. In his distress, he found his way to the Roslin Community, where Roland found him on his knees in prayer in the chapel. The young man poured out his story and unburdened his heart. At the end of their conversation, Roland simply put his arms around him and gave him a hug! That hug symbolized everything for the man. He knew he was loved, accepted, forgiven. He went back,

found a block of sandstone and carved out a figure of the two
Adams. They are kneeling, embracing one another. Christ lays
his head on the right shoulder of fallen Adam, and fallen Adam
lays his head on the right shoulder of Christ, the second Adam.
The only way in which one can distinguish between the two
Adams is by the nail prints in the hands of Christ. That sculptor
saw himself in fallen Adam, and in that symbolic hug he saw
himself accepted in Christ, the second Adam. There one sees
the Pauline theology of an Irenaeus—that what was lost in
Adam has been restored in Christ. That is the biblical concept
of "the one and the many"—that we, the many, can see
ourselves accepted by grace in Christ, the one mediator, who
fulfills God's purpose—to gather together all things in Christ,
the head (*anakephalaiōsis*)—the doctrine of "recapitulation."

Irenaeus used the metaphor of "the two hands of God" in
his criticism of the heretic Marcion. God our Father has two
hands—the Word and the Spirit—by whom he created and
redeemed the world. Marcion had taught that the creator God
of the Old Testament was different from the redeemer God of
the New Testament. No, according to Irenaeus, the God who
created this world (and Adam) has redeemed this world (with
Adam) by the same Word and the same Spirit. The one by
whom and for whom all things were created has taken our
humanity to redeem us—"to bring many sons to glory." It is
by these two hands that God gives himself to us in love to bring
us to intimate communion. We can extend that metaphor
further. Think of a hug. When we hug somebody whom we
love there is a double movement. We give ourselves to the
beloved, and in the same act by putting our arms around the
other, we draw that person close to our heart! That is a parable
of the double movement of grace, the God-humanward and
the human-Godward movement in the priesthood of Christ

and the ministry of the Spirit. In Christ, the Word made flesh, and in the Holy Spirit—his two hands—God our Father in grace gives himself to us as God. But in Jesus Christ, the Word made flesh, and in the Spirit we are led to the Father by the intercessions of Christ and the intercessions of the Spirit. We are lifted up by "the everlasting arms." As in the mediatorial ministry of Christ, the Spirit is the interceding Spirit, through whom Jesus Christ our ascended high priest presents us to the Father.

In the parable of the prodigal son, when the son returned from the far country, he was eager to buy his way back into his father's favor. He requested work: "Make me like one of your hired servants. But while he was still a long way off his father saw him and was filled with compassion for him; he ran to his son, threw his arms around him (hugged him) and kissed him" (Lk 15:19-20). He received him back joyfully. I think we can hear the son's response: "Daddy, I love you! It is wonderful to be back home!" And then, "Dad, I have been a fool!" It is a parable of "evangelical repentance"—the response to a father's love, not a condition for it. Is that not the meaning of grace?

Chapter Three

Baptism & the Lord's Supper —the Way of Communion

IN HIS LECTURES, *CHRISTOLOGY*,[1] DIETRICH BONHOEFfer made the plea that in theology we give priority to the question of *who* over *how*, and that we always seek answers to the question of *how* in terms of *who*. Our dogmatic starting point in theology should be: Who is God? Who is Jesus Christ?—"Who do men say that I am?"—Who is the Holy Spirit? In our pragmatic Western society in this technological age, our starting point so often is the problems of the world, of church and society—problems of race, the inner city, unemployment, poverty, violence, injustice. These are issues of such urgent importance that we give primacy to the question of how to solve them. We can too readily assume that Christianity is meaningful, useful, relevant, even true, only if it is seen to offer solutions to these practical problems. We can too readily subsume theology (as Ritschl did in the nineteenth century) under the category of means and ends. This is the weakness of so-called culture Protestantism. It sees religion as the means to realize the ends of culture—partly the legacy of the older Ritschlianism (as Bonhoeffer saw) and widespread in our churches today.

Professor Geoffrey Bromiley told me how one day, standing in the mountains of the Sierra Nevada in California, high above Yosemite Valley, he was gazing at the beauty of the scene—the cascading waterfalls, the gigantic sequoia redwood trees, the lake below—when someone beside him exclaimed: "Do you know, if they put a dam down there, they could flood this valley and irrigate the farms of central California!" This person was preoccupied with the question of how to find enough water to meet human needs! It shows the pragmatism of our culture, which evaluates our world in terms of utility, means and ends. Here were two people with the same perceptual field but with two totally different apperceptions. The one saw beauty and the other only utility. So it can be in the world of theology. We can be so preoccupied with the problems of humanity, of society, of individual need or the problems of the self, that we see the Gospel exclusively in terms of these issues. We adopt an anthropological starting point, and then seek to justify religion in terms of its pragmatic value or relevance for our contemporary self-understanding—offering programs, structures, organizations, machinery to deal with these problems and the countless calls for action. It is as though by doing something, becoming more efficient, we will be successful and find solutions. Bonhoeffer's plea to such a world is to give primacy to the question of *who* in our theology. He points out that, throughout the Bible, the indicatives of grace always precede the imperatives of law and obligation. It is only as we know *who* God is and *what* he has done and is doing that we can find appropriate answers

to the question of *how*, and then see the incredible relevance of
the gospel to every area of life.

What does this mean for our understanding of worship? If
someone asks me what is the use of going to church, what good
does it do me, what do I get out of it, how do I answer these
questions? It is as though someone asks me what the use is of
getting married, what good does it do me. If I answered such
questions by saying, "Well, it is very useful to get married! You
have someone to do the housework, the shopping, cook the
meals, etc.," it would clearly be a false view of marriage. No
woman wants to be merely a housekeeper, kept because of her
utility! There is only one supreme reason for getting married—
for love's sake, for the other's sake, for mutual love, self-giving,
a longing for intimate communion, and sharing of everything.
So in Christian worship, we worship God for God's sake; we
come to Christ for Christ's sake, motivated by love. An awareness of God's holy love for us, revealed in Jesus Christ, awakens
in us a longing for intimate communion—to know the love of
the Father and to participate in the life and ministry of Christ.
Worship in the Bible is always presented to us as flowing from
an awareness of who God is and what he has done: "I am the
God of Abraham, Isaac and Jacob . . . I have loved you and
redeemed you . . . I will be your God and you will be my people.
Therefore, this is how you will worship me." As we have seen,
worship in the Bible is an ordinance of grace, a covenantal form
of response to the God of grace, prescribed by God himself.
This is supremely true of the New Testament understanding of
worship, as the gift of participating through the Spirit in the
incarnate Son's communion with the Father and his mission
from the Father to the world, in a life of wonderful communion.

From the history of Christian thought—indeed from any
study of the history of religion—we can see that our doctrine

of God determines our understanding of worship and prayer. It is also true for our understanding of humanity, for our anthropology. The counterpart of seeing God as a sovereign individual Monad "out there" is a very individualistic concept of worship—"God and the soul, the soul and its God," as we saw in Harnack. The counterpart of a legalistic concept of God as the contract-God who rewards human merit is certain medieval doctrines of penance or works of supererogation, or false notions of the mass as a propitiatory sacrifice. It can also lead to the notion of a Protestant work ethic, a false activism, emphasis on prosperity as a motive for Christian giving or tithing, or setting criteria for evaluating success in churches and their ministers. It can even blend with certain forms of revivalism, to lead to an expectation that God is bound to bless us and pour out his Spirit if we use certain methods. That was the flaw in the Judaizing heresy in New Testament times, which Paul attacks in his exposition of grace in Galatians. But a trinitarian understanding of God, a God of grace as in the Bible, leads to a very different concept of worship and of our humanity. God is love. Love always implies a communion between persons, and we have seen that in our Christian doctrine of God. The Father loves the Son in the communion of the Spirit. The Son loves the Father in the communion of the Spirit. God has his being-in-communion. This triune God has in grace created us as male and female in his image, that we might find our true being in intimate communion with him and with one another. He created us for *communio* to be "co-lovers" (*condiligentes*), as John Duns Scotus expressed it in the thirteenth century.[2] Three hundred years before the Reformation, he was concerned to call the church back to the centrality of the doctrine of the Trinity, in a time when the prevailing concepts of God as the unmoved mover, the impassible God, or the lawgiver, owed more to Aristotle, Stoicism and Western jurisprudence than to the Bible. Duns Scotus went on to teach that, even if the Fall had not happened, the incarnation would still have taken place. It was his way of saying that Jesus Christ did not come only to save us from our sins, but supremely to bring to fulfillment the trinitarian purposes of grace in creation. We should find the fulfillment of our humanity in a life of community in the kingdom of God—our true being-in-communion with God and one another, sharing in God's love for the world as "co-lovers." John McLeod Campbell, another Scottish theologian, had a similar concern in the mid-nineteenth century. He distinguished between the retrospective and the prospective aspects of Christ's incarnation and atonement. Retrospectively, Christ came to save us from our past sin, from guilt, from judgment, from hell. But prospectively he came to bring us to sonship, to communion with God in the kingdom of God. He saw that Western theology has too often limited salvation to the retrospective aspect, seeing Christ as Savior of our humanity only in the context of the Fall. But in the New Testament the two are never separated: "When the fullness of time had come, God sent his Son, born of a woman, born under the law, in order to redeem those who were under law, so that we might receive adoption as children. And because you are children, God has sent the Spirit of his Son into our hearts, crying, *Abba*! Father!" (Gal 4:4-6 NRSV). It is that prospective vision we so need to recover today.

It is in this trinitarian way we have to see worship, as the fulfillment of God's purposes in creation and redemption, to bring us into a life of communion with himself and one another. The triune God is in the business of creating community, in such a way that we are never more truly human, never more truly persons, than when we find our true being-in-communion.

As we have seen in the New Testament, Christ is the real agent in worship, the *leitourgos*, our high priest, who by his vicarious atoning sacrifice for our sins, cleanses us and sanctifies us that he might lead us into the holy presence of the Father—the Holy of Holies. This is how we must understand both baptism and the Lord's Supper, through which we participate in what he has done for us, once and for all, and is continuing to do, when, at his command, we take the visible elements of water, bread and wine. Christ baptizes us by the Spirit that we might participate in his cleansing of our humanity and enter into his body, the communion of saints. At the Lord's Supper, he brings his passion to our remembrance and draws us into wonderful communion—holy communion—with the Father, with himself and with one another, proleptic of our life in the kingdom of God, nourishing our faith "till he come."

Baptism into Christ into a Life of Communion
Participating by the Spirit in the vicarious baptism of Christ. In any discussion of baptism, the first question to be asked is not who should be baptized—infants or adults or both—nor how it should be administered—by sprinkling, pouring or immersion—nor whether it may be repeated. These are important questions, but they can only be answered when we have first asked what the meaning of baptism is. What does it signify? The important thing is not the sign but the *reality signified*. Only when it is clear what is signified can we seek to answer these further practical questions. That is also important for New Testament exegesis on the subject, which must not be divorced from our understanding of the person and work of Christ in the whole witness of the New Testament. We must do depth exegesis. The questions of who and of what are prior to how.
  What is signified in baptism?

1. *It is a sign of the one work of the one God, Father, Son and Holy Spirit* in the fulfillment of his filial purpose "to bring many sons to glory." Why do we baptize in the triune name? Not just because of our Lord's missionary command in Matthew 28:19, but because these words enshrine the good news of grace. The mission of the church in the world is grounded in the mission of the Son and the Spirit from the Father to bring us to sonship and communion. Our Lord began his ministry for us in his vicarious baptism in the waters of the Jordan when, as the Son, he received from the Father the baptism of the Spirit for us in our humanity and set his face to the cross. His own baptism was trinitarian.

Karl Barth tells the story of an old lady who once went to the evangelist Kohlbrügge and asked him, "Tell me, sir, when were you converted?" The evangelist, knowing well that she was interested in the details of his Christian experience, replied, "Madam, I was converted nineteen hundred years ago when Jesus Christ died on a cross for my sins and rose again." He was concerned to point away from himself and his own faith to Jesus Christ. The decisive event for him was not primarily anything in his own experience, important as that may be, but that Jesus "suffered under Pontius Pilate, was crucified, dead, buried . . . the third day he rose again from the dead, he ascended into heaven." It was as though he said, "When Christ died long ago for me, I died, and when Christ rose again for me from the dead in the garden of Joseph of Arimathea, I rose again. When Christ ascended for me into heaven, I ascended in him, and now my life is hid with Christ in God." That is the true testimony of faith, the inner witness of the Spirit. In the words of the apostle, "We thus judge that if one died for all, then all died." Christ *for us* is prior to Christ *in us*. This is enshrined in the words from the French Reformed baptismal liturgy:

Little child, for you Jesus Christ has come, he has fought, he has suffered. For you he entered the shadow of Gethsemane and the horror of Calvary. For you he uttered the cry "It is finished!" For you he rose from the dead and ascended into heaven and there he intercedes—for you, little child, even though you do not know it. But in this way the word of the Gospel becomes true. "We love him, because he first loved us."

These words from the liturgy of the French Reformed Church express so simply and profoundly the doctrine of grace which is at the heart of a Reformed theology of baptism. Indeed, in the testimony of faith, three answers can be given to the question of when I became a Christian. Firstly, I have been a child of God from all eternity in the heart of the Father. Secondly, I became a child of God when Christ the Son lived, died and rose again for me long ago. Thirdly, I became a child of God when the Holy Spirit—the Spirit of adoption—sealed in my faith and experience what had been planned from all eternity in the heart of the Father and what was completed once and for all in Jesus Christ. There are three moments but only one act of salvation, just as we believe there are three persons in the Trinity, but only one God. We may never divorce any one from the other two. So Jesus commissioned the disciples to preach the gospel and to baptize "in the name of the Father and of the Son and of the Holy Spirit." Of these three moments, the second is the decisive one in the gospel of grace. *Christus pro nobis* is prior to *Christus in nobis*. "Little child, for you Jesus Christ has come!"

The work of salvation is from beginning to end the work of God. Baptism is the sign of what the triune God does. God forgives, God cleanses, God regenerates, God adopts, God sends the Spirit of his Son into our hearts whereby we cry:

"*Abba*, Father." Our response to this is to say amen in faith—our passive recipient response. There is nothing more passive than dying, being buried, being baptized.

2. *It is a sign of the covenant of grace*, in Reformed language. So the Westminster Confession calls it a "sign and seal of the covenant of grace, immediately instituted by God to represent Christ and his benefits." It is a sacrament of the gospel. "Go and preach the Gospel to every creature"—by word and sign. So St. Augustine called the sacraments "visible preaching." The covenant of grace is not a bilateral covenant which we make with God at this moment of time as though God's grace is contingent on our faith and decision. Baptism then would be a seal of my faith and my decision, a badge of my conversion. The good news is that God has made a covenant for us in Christ and sealed it with his blood, nineteen hundred years ago. It is a unilateral covenant of grace—a *diathēkē* not a *synthēkē*—but we are summoned through the Spirit to say amen to it in faith, and to participate in "Christ and his benefits." Baptism is an act of faith which sets forth that covenant made for us and our children in Christ so long ago.

3. *The act of baptism in water sets forth Christ's baptism for us.* Jesus spoke of his death on the cross as his *baptisma*: "I have a baptism to be baptized with, and what constraint I am under until the ordeal is over" (Lk 12:50). He says to the disciples, "Can you be baptized with the baptism I am baptized with?" (Mk 10:38). That is not just a metaphor for suffering! It is the reality at the heart of the gospel, signified by the rite of baptism. It is by his baptism for us—his cross, his atoning death and his resurrection—that he forgives and sanctifies and secures our sonship. The work of the Holy Spirit is to "seal" that in our hearts and call us to participate in it by a life of daily dying and rising with Christ. Baptism is the sacrament of cleansing and

forgiveness. But it is not the water, not the church, not the minister, not my faith, not my dying and rising, which forgives and heals. It is Christ who has done this for us and in us by the Spirit. So we are baptized "in the name of Christ"—not our own name—and we are baptized into a life of union with Christ, of dying and rising with Christ, into a life of communion.

The one baptism. So, our baptism sets forth the one baptism of Christ. Ephesians 4:5 speaks of "one Lord, one faith, one baptism" and the Nicene Creed says "We believe in . . . one baptism for the remission of sins." Whether we are Presbyterian, Methodist, Baptist, Anglican or Roman Catholic, we participate in one baptism. The concept of one baptism is derived not simply from these two statements but from our understanding of the gospel. What do we mean by the one baptism?

1. *The one baptism means Christ's baptism for us.* Christ commenced his ministry by being baptized by the Spirit in the waters of the Jordan into a life of conflict with evil. It led to his baptism in blood upon the cross—not for himself, but for us. When he saw the people going down into the river to be baptized by John, confessing their sins, submitting to the verdict of guilty (which is repentance), Jesus said to John, "Baptize me! I will submit to the verdict of guilty for them!" He identified himself with sinners, that he might take their place as their substitute under the judgment of God. So he marched to the cross to be baptized for us—to be "circumcised for us" (Col 2:11ff.). The gospel is that Christ was baptized in blood on the cross, once and for all, one for all, the one on behalf of the many, the many in the one. In this way, his death was our death, his burial our burial, his resurrection our resurrection— his baptism for us our baptism. If baptism sets forth the love of the Father, it is grounded in the substitution of the Son.

2. *The one baptism means Christ's baptism of us by the Holy Spirit*. The Christ who was baptized for us nineteen hundred years ago now comes to baptize us by the Spirit to make us members of his body, that we might participate in his sonship and communion with the Father. John the Baptist said, "I baptize you with water, . . . he will baptize you with the Holy Spirit. . . ." The Christ who was himself baptized for us in our humanity by the Holy Spirit in the Jordan, who was baptized in blood for us on the cross to secure our sonship, at Pentecost baptized the church by the same Spirit to make it his body in a corporate baptism. And he still baptizes us personally into union with himself by the Spirit of adoption whereby we too, by a shared baptism of the Spirit, can cry: "*Abba*, Father."

3. *The one baptism means incorporation into Christ*. The one Christ baptizes by the one Spirit *into the one body* that we might participate in all that he has done and is doing for us, that we might receive him with all his blessings. Christ is the agent in baptism and he baptizes us into a life of sonship, of service, of dying and rising with him in newness of life (Rom 6). He baptizes us into that life of communion for which we were created in the image of the triune God, to be co-lovers (*condiligentes*).

What is the sign of baptism? Water is the visible sign of washing. Ananias said to Paul: "Be baptized and wash away your sins . . ." (Acts 22:16). Paul speaks about "the washing of water by the word" (Eph 5:26), and the writer to the Hebrews about "having our hearts sprinkled . . . and our bodies washed with pure water" (Heb 10:22). Immersion, sprinkling and pouring as forms of washing are all good biblical symbols for cleansing, where the real cleansing is by the blood of Christ and the Spirit. Note that:

□ Baptism in water is a sign in the first instance, not of anything in us, but of Christ in the Spirit. It is not my faith which cleanses but Christ by the Spirit—the Christ in whom I believe.

❏ Baptism is a seal which marks out the individual personally as someone who belongs to Christ, to make a visible difference between the church and the world. "Little child, for you Jesus Christ has come. . . ." This is part of the significance of household baptisms in the New Testament and in missionary situations. In baptism we say, "We and our family belong to Christ . . . and have repudiated the world. . . ."

❏ The water exhibits not an absent Christ, but a Christ present according to his promise. The Christ who was baptized at Calvary in our place, as our substitute, is present today to baptize us by the Holy Spirit, in faithfulness to his promise: "Lo, I am with you . . . " Baptism is a participatory sign.

To whom should baptism be administered? The Reformed confessions said "believers and their children," generally quoting Acts 2:31: "The promise is to you and to your children. . . ." The practice of infant baptism, however, is not based on one text like that, which is capable of different interpretations, but on the meaning of the whole gospel. The covenant of grace, promised to Abraham and fulfilled in Christ, was for us and our children. Two things are important here: (a) Christ did not die for adults only! He died for adults and children . . . "Little child, for you . . ." (b) God's grace is not conditioned by anything in us, not even by our faith! Nevertheless, baptism must always be an act of faith in the Christ who died for us and our children. It is not a sign of our faith, but of the Christ in whom we believe. There is no faith in the little child. But in faith we say: ". . . for you, little child, even though you do not know it . . ."

In the practice of infant baptism, we believe that in faith we are doing something for the child, long before the child comes to faith, in acknowledgment of what Christ did for all of us nineteen hundred years before we were born. But in faith we pray that Christ in his faithfulness, and in his own time, will bring this child to personal faith. The efficacy of baptism is not in the rite or in the water, but in the faithfulness of Christ. It might be argued that there is not one explicit reference in the New Testament to a child being baptized. Have we any warrant then for doing it? If we require explicit texts for our practice, then there would be no warrant for women to come to the Lord's Table. There is no single explicit reference to that in the New Testament. Our warrant is not in isolated texts or precedents, but in the gospel itself. Christ died for men and women, adults and infants, and we acknowledge that in faith in baptism and at the Lord's Supper. If Christ died for all, then why not baptize all indiscriminately? No! The one baptism means that Christ baptizes us by the Spirit within the sphere of the Spirit—the church. The Spirit acts through the Word, where the Word is preached and heard and children are instructed. Faith, as the work of the Spirit, comes through the Word. So questions are put to parents: Do you believe . . . ? Do you promise to instruct this little one . . . ? Baptism thus marks the frontier between the church and the world. It is an evangelical sacrament which in a very wonderful way enshrines the whole gospel of grace, which is unconditionally free for us and our children, but which summons us and our children unconditionally to costly faith and discipleship. It enshrines the love of the Father, the substitution of the Son and the sovereign activity of the Spirit. So with joy we say with Luther: "I have been baptized!" (*Baptizatus sum!*).

The Lord's Supper
Participating by the Spirit in the life of the ascended Christ, our high priest, in memory and communion. Jesus' whole life was a

life of worship. Even as a boy he was found in the temple, in his "Father's house." He daily offered himself in prayer and communion in the service of God and of humanity, praying on the mountainside and at times of great crises in his life—at his baptism, when he called the twelve, in his "high priestly prayer" at the Last Supper, in the garden of Gethsemane, on the cross—offering to God in our humanity a life of unbroken obedience. He interpreted his own passion in the light of Psalm 110 and the servant songs of Isaiah in his willing acceptance of death. The whole life of Jesus is a life of self-offering to the Father on behalf of the world, culminating in the one true sacrifice of love and obedience on the cross. It alone is acceptable to God, for all people, for all nations, for all times—"the offering by which he has perfected for all times those who are sanctified" (Heb 10:4).

Father, Son and Holy Spirit.

1. According to the New Testament, that life of communion with the Father did not begin at Bethlehem. He who was the eternal Son of God by nature, enjoying eternal communion with the Father, became the Son of Man that we "sons and daughters of men" might become "sons and daughters of God" by grace and be drawn into the Son's communion with the Father, that through the Spirit we too might call God "Father." The eternal Word who was with God and who was God, the only begotten Son of the Father, who created all things, took our humanity and "tabernacled" among us, that we might see the glory of the Father, and ourselves become sons and daughters of God (Jn 1:11-14).

2. That life of worship and communion with the Father which Jesus fulfilled in our humanity did not end in death. Having offered for us a life of perfect obedience to the Father, culminating in the one perfect self-offering for all people and

all nations, Jesus rose from the dead and returned to the Father to intercede for us (Rom 8:34) as our great high priest (Heb 4:14). As the eternal mediator of an eternal covenant, he now appears on our behalf in the presence of God that we might be accepted as sons and daughters (Eph 2:13ff.; 1 Tim 2:1-6; Heb. 4:14, 7:25, 9:24).

So we distinguish a twofold ministry of Christ: (a) the once and for all earthly worship and self-offering of Christ, extending from his birth to his death; (b) his continuing heavenly ministry of worship and intercession inaugurated by his resurrection and ascension. "Inasmuch as he is the great High Priest, Jesus fulfills then a double ministry: on the one hand that of the expiatory act accomplished once and for all; on the other hand, the ministry of extending and exploiting the full benefits of his saving work which lasts into eternity."[3]

3. Jesus draws men and women into his life of communion with the Father by the Spirit, putting his prayer "Father" on our lips, sharing his sonship with us. In both his earthly and continuing heavenly ministry, through his Spirit, he makes the Father known to us by sharing his unique knowledge of the Father. He teaches us to pray, draws us into eternal communion with the Father by uniting us in communion with himself, and creates a reconciled community among men and women. So we are graciously given the gift of worshiping the Father, in and through the Son, in the communion of the Holy Spirit in the communion of saints praying "in the name of Jesus," "through Jesus Christ our Lord." So we are baptized in the name of the Father, the Son and the Holy Spirit into the community which worships the Father, in and through the Son, in the communion of the Spirit. Confessing faith in the Trinity (as in the Apostles' Creed), we receive the blessing of God, Father, Son and Holy Spirit.

Christ's worship is our worship—in the communion of the Spirit. Jesus Christ, our risen and ascended Lord, draws us into himself, into his life of prayer in the presence of the Father—in an act of memory, in a life of communion—through the Holy Spirit.

1. *Participation.* Jesus taught us to call God "Father" and in our prayers to say "Our Father . . ." All true prayer is gathered up in that one word. Jesus not only taught us to pray "Father," but is himself the living embodiment of that prayer. In his earthly life of communion with the Father, in a life lived in the Spirit, we are given a glimpse (cf. Jn 17) into the eternal life of the Trinity. The Son of God became our brother that he might lift us up into that life of wonderful communion, and so he sends his Spirit into our hearts and puts his prayer on our lips whereby we too can pray "*Abba*, Father." So in the communion of the Spirit in the communion of saints, our prayers on earth are the echo of his prayers in heaven. By grace we are given to participate in his intercession for all humanity. So in our corporate worship we are called to be a royal priesthood, bearing in our hearts the sorrows and cares and tragedies of our world as our heavenly High Priest does. By grace we are given to participate in the life, ministry, sufferings, death, resurrection and continual intercessions of him who is the head of the body.

2. *Memory.* Jesus said to his disciples, "I will pray the Father, and he will give you another Comforter . . . and He will bring all things to your remembrance." At the Last Supper, Jesus said, "This do in remembrance of me." The word *anamnēsis* is of a rich liturgical significance in the Bible and generally in worship—we speak of "remembering people in prayer," calling upon God to remember his world, of sacraments as "memorials" of Christ, or of Christ as the living Memorial.

The word does not simply denote recollecting some remote

date of bygone history, as every schoolchild remembers A.D. 1066 or 1492. Rather, it means remembering in such a way that we see our participation in the past event and see our destiny and future as bound up with it. For example, when the Jews in their worship remember the Passover and the exodus from Egypt, they do not think of it as simply an irretrievable date from over three thousand years ago. Rather, they remember it in such a way that they confess: "We were once Pharaoh's bondsmen, but by the grace of God, we are the people whom God brought up out of the land of Egypt. We are the people whom God delivered from slavery and made a free people and with whom God has made his covenant saying: 'I will be your God and you shall be my people.' That mighty act of God was our redemption." Thus Israel lives by this kind of historical memory. At the present point in her historical existence, she stands related to that historical point of departure as an elect covenanted people in the faithfulness of her ever-present Lord. This is what gives her her historical continuity and sense of identity through the centuries, and why in her cult, in the *Haggadah* (the telling of the paschal story) and the *Hallels* (singing of praise for the deliverance of the exodus) she recapitulates the saving acts of God. "In cultic remembrance . . . the past is rendered present; thus it is re-present-ation of the past so that it lives again in the present time. This, for lack of a better word, we may call a presentifying of the past."[4]

So at the Lord's Table we do not merely remember the passion of our Lord as an isolated date from nineteen hundred years ago. Rather, we remember it in such a way that we know by the grace of God we are the people for whom our Savior died and rose again, we are the people whose sins Jesus confessed on the cross, we are the people with whom God has made a new covenant in the blood of Christ, we are the Israel of God to whom God has said "I will be your God and you shall be my people." We, today, are the people whose sorrows and cries Jesus bears on his kingly heart as he intercedes for us and constitutes himself the eternal Memorial for all his creatures before God. We are what we are today by the grace of God, because of what God did for us then.

This work of memory, of realizing our participation and fellowship in the sufferings of Christ, is the work of the Holy Spirit. He brings these things to our remembrance and interprets to us the meaning of the events. We remember Christ— yet it is not so much we who remind ourselves of these events, but Jesus Christ, who brings his passion to our remembrance through the Holy Spirit, as our ever-living and ever-present Lord, who, in his own person, is our memorial in the presence of the Father. In other words, our memorial is the earthly counterpart of the heavenly memorial. Christ, in constituting himself as our memorial before the Father, by his Spirit, lifts us up as we present our memorials before God. So the Lord's Supper, like the Passover, is a memorial to us, but also a memorial before God.

Prayer is likewise described in the New Testament as a memorial before God. So in Acts 10:4 the angel says to Cornelius, "Your prayers and your alms are come up for a memorial (*eis mnēmosynon*) before God." This may reflect the priestly ministry of vicarious prayer and loving concern where we bear the burdens and needs of others on our hearts before God. The background of this concept of prayer may be the liturgical prayers of the high priest in Old Testament Israel. He presented the prayers of Israel before God, carrying the names of the tribes of Israel on his breastplate "as a memorial" (Ex 28:12).

So the church as a royal priesthood is called in the name of

Christ and under Christ to be a living memorial. By bearing the needs of the world on our hearts, both in intercessory prayer and in social concern, we call for the Father to remember all his creatures—and are a constant reminder to the world that this world is Christ's by right of creation and redemption.

3. *Communion.* The Christ whom we remember is not an absent Christ. He is present in the power of the Spirit to bring the things we celebrate to our remembrance in an act of communion. Corresponding to the twofold ministry of Christ, the earthly and the heavenly, there is a twofold ministry of Christ through the Spirit: (a) to bring the things of his once and for all earthly ministry to our remembrance; (b) to lift up our hearts and minds in the *sursum corda* into his communion with the Father, to make us participants of the new humanity in him. The Christ who meets us at the table, on the one hand, is the one in whose representative humanity our broken humanity was assumed and judged, the one in whose self-consecration and self-offering we were consecrated and healed. On the other hand, he is the ascended Lord in whose continuing humanity our humanity is presented by our great high priest to the Father, the one by whose eternal Spirit we are given by grace to share in the substitutionary self-presentation of Christ in the Holy of Holies. The one who is truly present in the power of the Spirit in the eucharistic parousia is also the ascended one who is absent. So Calvin used to say, Christ is *quodammodo praesens et quodammodo absens*, in a manner present and yet in a manner absent. The Christ who draws us into such wonderful communion is the whole Christ, the God-man, in whom and through whom God and humanity are reconciled. God and humanity are one in him, our mediator, who summons us to be reconciled to one another and who sends us out in mission to be ambassadors of the gospel of reconciliation to the ends

of the earth and to the end of the age.

The Holy Spirit, through whom we participate in the person and ministry of Christ, exercises a twofold ministry which in a further way corresponds to the twofold ministry of Christ— namely, of *representing God to humanity* and of *representing humanity to God*. It is in this twofold sense we are to interpret the work of the Spirit in taking the things of Christ and ministering them to us: (a) Through the Holy Spirit God comes to meet us in worship, in the ministry of word and sacrament, and summons us to respond in faith and obedience and thanks-giving, in offering ourselves to God as a living sacrifice, which is our "reasonable worship." This is the one side of the dialogue, the communion, which is worship. (b) In our human, frail, broken, unworthy response, the Spirit helps us in our infirmi-ties, lifting us up to Christ who, in his ascended *humanity*, is our God-given response, the leader of our worship, the pioneer of our faith, our advocate and high priest, who through the eternal Spirit presents us with himself to the Father. So in and through the mediatorial ministry of the Spirit, we worship the Father in the name of Christ: "For we know not what we should pray for as we ought; but the Spirit himself makes intercession for us with groanings which cannot be uttered. And he who searches the hearts knows what is the mind of the Spirit, because he makes intercession for the saints according to the will of God" (Rom 8:22-27). That is, the Spirit is not only speaking Spirit but also interceding Spirit, exercising not only a prophetic ministry but also a priestly ministry. It is all too possible for us in the Reformed tradition so to stress (a) that we neglect (b). We so stress that God comes to us as God to address us through his Word in preaching that we short-circuit the real humanity of Christ, the role of the continuing priesthood of Christ in representing us to God, and have a one-sided view of the work of the Spirit. We can then so obtrude our own response to the Word in Pelagian fashion that we obscure or forget the God-given response made for us by Jesus Christ. It is possible for us so to obtrude our own offering of praise that we lose sight of the one true offering of praise made for us (Heb 2:12). We then lose sight of the earlier Reformed understanding of the Lord's Supper which we find in Calvin or Knox or in the communion sermons of Robert Bruce in the older Scottish tradition. We would also lose much of the comfort of the gospel. God does not throw us back upon ourselves to make our response to the Word in our own strength. But graciously he helps our infirmities by giving us Jesus Christ and the Holy Spirit to make the appropriate response for us and in us. Can we not adapt Galatians 2:20 and say, "We pray, and yet it is not we who pray, but Christ who prays for us and in us; and the prayers which we now offer in the flesh, we offer by the faithfulness of the one who loved us and offered himself for us"?

Christ's worship is our worship—through a wonderful exchange. The Christian gospel is a gospel of reconciliation, a concept enshrined at the heart of all worship. God in his grace in reconciling us to himself, lifts us up into a life of wonderful communion by effecting a wonderful exchange. So the apostle says in 2 Corinthians 5:18-21, "God was in Christ, reconciling the world to himself." How has he done it? "Christ was innocent of sin, and yet for our sake God made him one with the sinfulness of men so that we might be made one with the goodness of God himself."

As Calvin argued in book 4 of the *Institutes*, this is the heart of the theology of the sacraments, particularly the Lord's Supper, which so enshrines the *mirifica commutatio*, the "wonderful exchange"—that Christ took what was ours that he might give us what is his. He takes our broken sinful humanity and cleanses it by his self-sanctifying life of communion with the Father, his obedience, death and resurrection. And now he comes back to us in the power of the Spirit to give himself to us in an act where he gives us back our humanity, now renewed in him, saying: "Take, eat, this is my body which is broken for you." Our reception of Christ is our grateful acknowledgment of this wonderful exchange. The body on which we feed is the body which he assumed for our sakes, that in our worship we might be sanctified by the once and for all self-offering of Christ. In the communion of the Spirit, in virtue of this exchange, we know that his humanity is our humanity so graciously assumed, his death our death which we show forth, his life our life till he comes, his self-offering our offering, his communion with the Father our communion into which he lifts us up by his Spirit. The Lord's Supper, as an evangelical ordinance, enshrines very vividly the inner meaning of the gospel (*Institutes* 4.17.2).

Calvin is here spelling out, not only the meaning of the evangel, but also the meaning of the Greek word for reconciliation. The Greek word *katallassein* means quite literally "to effect an exchange," "to buy" something, "to exchange one thing for another." So it comes to mean "to reconcile," to exchange friendship for enmity, love for hatred, peace for hostility. That, says the apostle, is what God has done for us in Christ. Jesus came to take our enmity to himself that he might give us love and forgiveness in exchange, to take our sins that he might give us righteousness in exchange, to take our death that he might give us eternal life in exchange. So we humbly and joyfully receive him, "clothed with all his benefits."

Consecration and communion. Jesus effected this wonderful exchange to share with us his wonderful communion with the Father. This is enshrined in the order of the communion service.

When we come to the Lord's Table to worship, we come to offer ourselves to the Lord. But what can we render to the Lord, for our lives are so unworthy, so broken and so sinful? After the preaching of the word, the bread and wine are brought in and set before our eyes and consecrated—not as a sign of our self-offering to the Lord, but as a memorial that nineteen hundred years ago the Son of God assumed our life. He assumed our body of flesh, our mind, our spirit, sinful though they be, sanctified them in his own person, and in our name made that Offering which we could never make. Indeed our self-offering, for a moment, is set aside that we might remember the great offering made for us. But the service does not end there. That same Christ, who is our eternal offering in the heavens, now comes to us in an act of self-giving and says: "Take, eat, this is my body which is for you." He lifts us with our self-offering of praise and thanksgiving into communion with himself. He gives back our life to us, converted and regenerated in him. Is it not for these evangelical reasons that communion follows consecration? Again adapting Galatians 2:20, we might say at the Lord's Table, "We offer ourselves to the Lord, and yet it is not we who offer, but Christ who has offered himself for us and who is our offering, and the offering which we now make in the flesh we make by the faithfulness of him who loved us and gave himself for us."

"We offer . . . and yet it is not our offering. It is Christ's." This is what, in intention at least, Rome seeks to say in the Mass. "It is bread . . . and yet suddenly we know it is not bread. It is Christ!" There is an evangelical intention. But from our Reformed point of view the old medieval doctrine of transubstantiation said it in the wrong way. It made the moment of *conversio* what takes place in the elements, in the act of consecration—no doubt as the act of God in the action of the priest. But this obscures, in too Pelagian a fashion, the heart of the gospel of grace that the real *conversio* of our humanity took place in the substitutionary self-consecration of Jesus. In his life, death and resurrection, in the once and for all action of our one high priest, we participate through the Spirit, who renews us in the image of God. Calvin and Robert Bruce could speak of a "conversion" in the "use" of the elements, in their being set apart from all common use to this holy use and mystery, but not in the sense of a change in the elements themselves.

At the Last Supper, Jesus took bread and said, "This is my body" (*hoc est corpus meum*). Deep divisions have occurred in the Christian church over the interpretation of these words between the Roman Catholic, the Lutheran and Reformed traditions—a debate which still continues and is still sadly a cause of division. But what is significant is that for 450 years these three main traditions of Western Christianity have held two things in common. First, we are united in believing in the real presence of Jesus Christ. We do not worship an absent Christ. The feast is not a mere memorial of the death of Christ, as a past event—a weakness in the experience model we discussed earlier. Secondly, we are united in believing that we commune with the whole Christ, not with a "naked" Christ (*nudus Christus*), as Luther put it, a divine Christ shorn of his humanity. We do not merely commune with the Son of God as the second person of the Trinity but with the incarnate Lord.[5] In the language we have used, it is Jesus Christ our great high priest who, in our humanity, is the one true worshiper who lifts us up to share in his communion with the Father, who constitutes us a royal priesthood to share in his worship and vicarious self-offering. So often when theologians have sought to express how Jesus Christ, the whole Christ, is present, differences have occurred—doctrines of transubstantiation, consubstantiation, or a Reformed emphasis on Christ as "in a manner present and yet in a manner absent" (*quodammodo praesens et quodammodo absens*—Calvin). The question of *how* is not unimportant, but we must always seek answers in terms of *who*. For example, how do we express a doctrine of the real presence of Christ together with his eschatological absence in his risen humanity—as the ascended Lord, whom we remember and show forth "till he come"? We must not so stress his real presence that we lose sight of his (eschatological) absence, nor so stress absence as to lose his real presence. Here the doctrine of the Holy Spirit is important for interpreting the now and the not yet. Jesus Christ is present in the power of the Spirit, but the same Spirit keeps us in suspense (*suspensio*). The end is not yet. Now we are the children of God, enjoying real communion with Jesus Christ, the whole Christ. It does not yet appear what we shall be, but when he appears we shall be like him, and enjoy endless communion with him. But to say that Christ is present in the power of the Spirit does not mean that we simply feed upon Christ spiritually, in some metaphorical sense. Indeed, it is not so much that we feed upon Christ by faith but that he is truly present in the power of the Spirit to feed us and unite us with himself in his communion with the Father in his heavenly intercessions.

Once again, in Bonhoeffer's language, we need to give primacy to the question of *who* over *how*. More important than understanding the mode of his presence is the awareness of who this Christ is who is present. What has he done once and for all? What is he continuing to do for us in his vicarious humanity as our high priest as he nourishes his one body, and draws us to the Father and to one another in communion—for "we being many are one loaf." When we focus on the question of who, we can rejoice together as we look away from ourselves to him, that he may sanctify us and lead us together into the presence of the Holy Father.

It was highly significant that in the B.C.C. Commission there was a common concern to return to the great doctrine of the Trinity, to discover our oneness in Christ, for a better common understanding of worship, that God might fulfill in us and through us, by his grace, his wonderful purposes of communion—that we might be, in Duns Scotus's word, "co-lovers" (*condiligentes*), participating together in the very life of God and in his love for the world.

Chapter Four

Gender, Sexuality & the Trinity

I HAVE BEEN CONCERNED TO STRESS THE NEED TO RE-cover the centrality of the doctrine of the Trinity in the life of our churches today for a number of reasons—for a better doctrine of God as a covenant God, not a contract-God; for a more biblical understanding of worship; and for a less individualistic anthropology—an understanding of our humanity and our destiny in the purposes of the God of grace, to be a community of persons enjoying communion with God and with one another. It is encouraging that so many theologians today are pointing in this direction, as in the B.C.C. Commission, calling churches back to "the forgotten Trinity." But there are voices pointing in a counter-direction.

An issue widely discussed in many churches throughout the world is the question, raised not least by the feminist movement, about the language we use for God. When we talk about God as Father and Son and speak about the Son of God becoming Son of Man that we "sons of men" might become "sons of God by grace," is this not the result of projecting male, sexist, patriarchal language onto God? Is this not the product of a male-dominated culture, both in the Bible and down the centuries? If we may use masculine language, it is asked, can we not also use feminine language and feminine images of God, and add the concept of motherliness to express more fully the love and compassion in the heart of God? Also, there is the proper concern to use inclusive language in our worship.

As I have lectured and preached in different parts of the world in recent years, I have seen churches and colleges very deeply divided on this issue in New Zealand, Australia, Canada and the USA. In November 1993, a conference was held in Minneapolis, Minnesota, as part of the Decade of the Church in Solidarity with Women, on the subject of "Re-Imagining God, Community and the Church," with the explicit call for new images of God to express the concerns of women in our male-dominated society. Over two thousand people from 27 countries attended, including most of the major denominations—Presbyterians, Methodists, Episcopalians, Lutherans, Baptists, Roman Catholics. The largest number (409) came from the Presbyterian Church, USA, which contributed some $66,000 to run the conference. Such extreme statements were made at that conference, calling into question so much traditional trinitarian language for God, that it roused widespread concern and indignation across the USA. As a result, $11 million were withheld from central Presbyterian Church funds, largely by evangelical churches. It is not my concern here to comment on the details of that conference, but only to note that it raised the whole question of the adequacy of trinitarian language for God. The result was that, when the General Assembly of the Presbyterian Church, USA, met at Wichita in

Kansas in June 1994, it received overtures of complaint from over 50 presbyteries and sessions with thousands of letters of protest. In response the Assembly acknowledged that

so many members of churches were offended, dismayed, hurt and angered because they believe that the P.C. (USA) either no longer adheres to its traditional theological moorings or is afraid to say that it does. Our response to these presbyteries is to affirm joyfully and gratefully our Presbyterian confessional standards, particularly those standards which were criticized and ridiculed at the conference:

We affirm the one triune God.

We affirm the uniqueness of God's incarnation in Jesus Christ.

We affirm the death and resurrection of Jesus Christ for our salvation.

We affirm that the Scriptures, by the Holy Spirit, are the unique and authoritative witness to Jesus Christ.

We affirm again and again the faith once delivered and historically expressed in the Nicene and Apostles' Creeds, and the other historic confessions of our church.

We reject teachings that deny the tenets of our faith. Let there be no doubt that theology matters, that our Reformed tradition is precious to us, and that we intend to hand it down to the next generation, to our children and our grandchildren.

This statement was passed by 98.9 per cent in favor with only four dissenting voices. It was a very powerful and important statement in the contemporary situation of the church, affirming the uniqueness of Jesus Christ and the trinitarian nature of our faith and worship.

But I would make two comments. Firstly, it seems to me it is not enough to assert these great doctrines without being concerned to understand them and to help our churches, not least our lay members, to realize their importance in an age when both the uniqueness of Jesus Christ and the trinitarian nature of our faith and worship are so under attack. Yes, theology matters! Secondly, the church must bring out into the open the theological issues which are at stake, lay bare the presuppositions of those who are attacking them and reply to those. The issues will not go away, as I have heard some leading church people say. We cannot dismiss the opposition and push the issues under the carpet. The church in all ages has had to contend for her faith. The doctrine of the Trinity is the grammar of the church's faith and worship.

The subject is a vast one, and all we can do here is to show some of the theological issues which are at stake. These must be raised if our churches are not to be deeply divided, and if we are to contend for the gospel of grace and for the trinitarian nature of our faith and of the Church as a worshiping community, called to participate by the Spirit in the Son's communion with the Father and the Son's mission from the Father to the world.

The Arian-Nicene Debate Today

Not long ago I was lecturing on the theology of worship in a college which was deeply divided theologically, partly because certain members of the teaching staff were extreme liberal feminists. A male student in the class asked me, "Are you not being sexist in believing in the Trinity, and speaking of God as Father, Son and Holy Spirit, and asserting that the Son of God became Son of Man?" I replied by saying that, first of all, he had asked me a very important question. How do we use any language for God—how can we call him good, loving, faithful, or just? This raises all the questions of analogy, metaphor, simile, parable, allegory, etc., which have been discussed down the centuries and which are more important today than ever. Secondly, the subject he had raised was discussed in depth in what was perhaps the greatest debate in the history of the church—between the Nicene Fathers and the followers of Arius—leading to the Nicene Creed, the most important ecumenical creed ever formulated.

What was that debate all about? The Arians denied the doctrine of the Trinity and the deity of Christ. Arius asked the question, "What do we mean by 'father' and 'son'?" I explained to the class that I have a son called Alan. There was a time when I was not a father. Then my wife conceived and Alan was born. I became a father. Likewise, there was a time when my son was not. He came into existence when my wife conceived and he was born. If you define "father" and "son" in those biological, sexual terms and then project them onto God, as Arius did, then you will argue quite consistently that there was a time when God was not Father. He only became Father when he created the Son. Likewise, there was a time when the Son was not. He only came into existence when God created him. So Arius denied the doctrine of the Trinity and, in fact, rarely spoke of God as Father. Likewise, he argued that the Son of God was a creature, so denying the deity of Christ. The Nicene Fathers replied, "That is not what we mean by Father and Son. He is eternally Father, eternally begetting and the Son is eternally the Son, eternally begotten, not made"—as in the words of the Nicene Creed. Athanasius said to Arius, "You are a mythologizer (*mythologein*), projecting your own images on to God. We do not engage in mythology, but in theology (*theologein*)."[1]

What did Athanasius understand the task of theology to be? In Matthew 23:8, Jesus is recorded as saying to the disciples, "Do not call anyone on earth 'father,' for you have one Father, and he is in heaven. . . . The greatest among you will be your servant." What is our Lord saying? He is recognizing that the word "father" is a patriarchal, sexist one in a culture where men dominate women and often use them simply as servants or sex objects. Jesus is saying that God is not like that! He is evacuating the word of all male, sexist, patriarchal connotations in calling God "Father." He says elsewhere: "Anyone who has seen me, has seen the Father" (Jn 14:9). "All things have been committed to me by my Father." "No one knows the Son except the Father, and no one knows the Father except the Son and those to whom the Son chooses to reveal him" (Mt 11:27). Jesus alone truly knows the Father, and his mission from the Father is to make the Father known. He does so by taking the form of a servant and by living a life of loving obedience, going to the cross. Fatherhood is then defined for us by Jesus on the cross. We are not thrown back on ourselves to project our biological, sexist images of "father" onto God—to "mythologize." The Christian church has never simply called God "Father," but always "the Father of our Lord Jesus Christ," and he is "the Father from whom his whole family in heaven and on earth derives its name" (Eph 3:14ff.). In theology our knowledge of God as Father is derived from his self-revelation in Jesus Christ. The danger of certain extreme liberal feminists is that they evacuate the word "Father" of all the content Jesus has put into it, and then want to dismiss the word as sexist and patriarchal—in effect accusing Jesus of being a mythologizer. To return to the question in class, I then said that, if they accused me of being sexist in talking about the Trinity, were they not accusing me of being an Arian? But perhaps they were the Arians if they insisted that the word is a patriarchal, biological, sexist one. Far from being sexist, the doctrine of the Trinity is the opposite. The ancient church hammered out the doctrine, as in the

Nicene Creed, against any sexist notions. They were clear that there is no gender in God; but, in revealing himself, God has commandeered human language and named himself as "Father." It is a name, not just a human metaphor and certainly not one we project on to God. But as such it has to be interpreted analogically in comparing it and contrasting it with human fatherhood, and doing so in the light of the life and ministry of Jesus Christ. This is the task of theology.[2]

The Nicene debate seems to me to be of fundamental importance today, in the light of accusations that talk of God as Father, Son and Holy Spirit is sexist, with male images projected onto God by a male-dominated, sexist culture.[3] The contention, therefore, is that we need new images of God, for example, female images. This was the basic theme of the Minneapolis Conference on "Re-Imagining God, Community and the Church," and behind the proposal that *Sophia* (the Greek feminine word for wisdom) be used to describe the object of our worship, and prayers be offered to her as our Mother.

The presupposition behind this extreme liberal approach is that God is unknown. We must explore the depths of our own experience and spirituality to find images and language with which to describe God or to account for moral and religious experience. This was the basic presupposition of Arius in the ancient world, and of Immanuel Kant and his successors today, from Schleiermacher to Bultmann and to the antirealism of Don Cupitt. We might express it summarily in a diagram as found in figure 4—what I have called the Protestant liberal model.

Right and Wrong Roads in the Feminist Debate
Behind this contemporary demand by many feminists for new

UNKNOWN GOD	UNKNOWN GOD	UNKNOWN GOD	UNKNOWN GOD
|	|	|	|
JESUS	PAUL	ARIUS-KANT	US

1. GOD TALK
   - our cultural projection
   - expression of self-understanding
   - culturally relative
   - mythology

2. MORALS
   - relative
   - my choice, our mutual consent
   - expression of my (our) self-understanding
   - criterion—personal (mutual) self-realization
   - culturally relative

i.e. nothing given by God
    no revelation
    subjective experience is criterion
    all is relative—no absolutes
TASK = Explore my own spirituality

Figure 4. The Protestant Liberal Model

images of God, there is a very genuine legitimate protest and a cry for justice. There is the fact that for centuries—from the very beginning?—the church has been largely male-dominated, patriarchal, hierarchical. Women have been excluded from the ordained ministry and from holding certain offices. The false argument has been used that only a man can represent a male Jesus. But this portrays an inadequate understanding of the incarnation. The Son of God, in assuming our humanity, became a man, not to sanctify maleness, but our common humanity so that, be we men or women, we can see the dignity and beauty of our humanity sanctified in him.

Furthermore, so many women have been used, abused, discarded, hurt, divorced, exploited economically and sexually by men down through the centuries, that there is a rising tide of resentment, anger, bitterness and even hatred of men, with a legitimate demand for justice and equality. So many women have had unfortunate experiences in their own homes that the word "father" conjures up ugly images. So often, tragically, the only dad some children know is an alcoholic or one who has abused his wife and family. This makes it all the more important that we allow Jesus Christ to interpret true fatherhood for us, both human and divine. We think of the Pauline injunction: "With eyes wide open to the mercies of God, I beg you, my brothers, as an act of intelligent worship, to give him your bodies, as a living sacrifice, consecrated to him and acceptable by him. Don't let the world around you squeeze you into its own mold, but let God remold your minds from within, so that you may prove in practice that the plan of God for you is good, meets all his demands and moves toward the goal of true maturity" (Rom 12:1-2, J. B. Phillips). We need to let God remold our concepts of Father and Son as we contemplate the mystery of the Father-Son relationship given to us in Jesus Christ in the New Testament witness.

As we reflect on the history of Christian thought, we can see that the word "Father" has been wedded often to wrong concepts of God as the unmoved mover, the impassible God, a static substance with impersonal attributes, or as the lawgiver understood in terms of the concept of *lex*, the law of contract, of Western jurisprudence and politics, with its roots in Stoicism—the contract-God who will only be gracious if there is human merit. No wonder highly unsatisfactory images of God as Father can arise! What is so often wrong is not the word "Father" but the baggage that can be put into it. Hence again the call of so many contemporary theologians and churches to recover "the forgotten Trinity." Theology matters. If the church neglects this task, we shall witness a sweeping wave of neo-Arianism, with the unitarian, human-centered worship which goes with it at the altar of the "unknown God."

It seems to me that the right approach for the church to adopt in seeking women's liberation is to take a stand on the incarnation. To hold out Jesus Christ to the world is not only to hold out personal salvation and eternal life in our evangelism, but it is also to give all people their humanity. Whatever else the incarnation means, it is that all people and all races—Jew or Gentile, black or white, male or female—are meant to see their humanity assumed by Christ, sanctified by his life in the Spirit of unbroken communion with the Father, by his death and resurrection, offered to the Father "without spot or wrinkle," and given back to them in the mission of the church. There should be no divorce between evangelism and humanization in the church's witness to Jesus Christ. Women are meant to find in Christ and receive from the church the full dignity and beauty of their humanity, equally with men. Tragically the church has been so often "molded," not by Jesus Christ, but by the patterns of a patriarchal culture.

Likewise, we are meant to interpret our humanity, our male-female relations, in the light of the Trinity. God is love. Love always implies communion between persons, and that is what we see supremely in God. The Father loves the Son in the communion of the Spirit. The Son loves the Father in the communion of the Spirit in their continuing mutual "indwelling" (*perichōrēsis* was the Greek word used by the fathers of the church). The Spirit is the bond of communion between the Father and the Son and between God and ourselves. The Spirit is God giving God's self in love. The Father and the Son and the Spirit are equally God (*autotheoi*). But there is differentiation within God—personal distinctions in the Godhead. There is unity, diversity and perfect harmony. It is this triune God who has being-in-communion, in love, who has created us as male and female in that image to be "co-lovers" (*condiligentes* in

Duns Scotus's expressive word[4]), to share in the triune love and to love one another in perichoretic unity. "Then God said, 'let us make man in our image, in our likeness.' . . . So God created man in his own image, in the image of God he created him: male and female he created them" (Gen 1:26-27).[5] These purposes of God in creation find their fulfillment in redemption. Therefore, to understand what it means to be in the image of God, one must look at Christ and the new creation in him. "There is neither Jew nor Greek, slave nor free, male nor female, for you are all one in Christ Jesus" (Gal 3:28). This does not mean that it does not matter, therefore, whether we are male or female. We do not become unisex. If so, what would be the difference between heterosexuality and homosexuality? There is unity, diversity and harmony which should be reflected in the church. The gospel does not eliminate our gender identity. But as men and women we find our masculine and feminine identity and fulfillment in Christ, our true being in mutual communion.

In the first epistle of Peter we read: "Slaves, submit yourselves to your masters . . ." (2:18). Further on we read: "Wives, in the same way, be submissive to your husbands" (3:1). It took the church over eighteen hundred years to get rid of slavery, to recognize the significance of that other text that in Christ there is neither slave nor free. It is apparently taking two thousand years to recognize that in Christ there is neither male nor female and to give to women their full equality with men. To understand what it means to be in the image of God, we must look at Jesus Christ, not at fallen humanity. In the beginning it was after the Fall that God said to the woman, "I will greatly increase your pains in childbearing: with pain you will give birth to children. Your desire will be for your husband and he will rule over you" (Gen 3:16). Great misuse has been made of that text. It is descriptive of the tragic results of the Fall. It is not prescriptive for God's good purposes in creation. As we look together as men and women to Jesus Christ, the one by whom and for whom we were all created, we know we are one in him, subject to one another in him, and are equal in him. This is particularly important in any discussion of the ministry of women in the church. Our starting point should be the sole priesthood of Jesus Christ. There is only one true priest in the church, in the one body. In Christ there is neither male nor female. Christ calls men and women into his royal priesthood, the church, to participate by the Spirit in his ministry—the one prophet, priest and king—and gives spiritual gifts to every member of his body, to women as well as men, for edifying the body. The church derives her structures from Christ, not from isolated texts of Holy Scripture taken out of context, nor from a male-dominated hierarchical tradition. As I see it, a proper doctrine of the Trinity, the incarnation, the sole priesthood of Christ, our understanding of the new creation in Christ, commits us to radical feminism, carefully defined.

The wrong road for feminists to take in seeking women's liberation is to attack the doctrines of the Trinity and the incarnation, to reject the view that God has revealed himself—named himself as "Father" through the person of the Son—and instead to explore their own feminine spirituality to create new images of God. That was the road of ancient gnosticism. We referred earlier to Allan Bloom's *The Closing of the American Mind* and his thesis that, when belief in God and the objectivity of moral law recedes in our Western democracy in a secular age, the individualism out of which it grew can collapse into a narcissistic preoccupation with the self—with self-fulfillment, self-realization, self-esteem, the human potential movement. Religion can then become a means toward self-realization as seen in extreme form in the neo-gnosticism of the New Age movement, where the self is identified with God, as in the antirealism of Don Cupitt. The task then becomes to know yourself. Realize your own identity. We can discover God in the depths of our own spirituality. It is in this climate that there arises the cry for new images of God which will express our own self-understanding and sexuality. At the Re-Imagining Conference, in preparing a woman's litany, a radical feminist declared, "I found God in myself and I loved her. I loved her fiercely," and "New gods arise when they are needed!" A liturgy was prepared—a service where milk and honey, female symbols, rather than bread and wine, were used in the celebration of the goddess Sophia and of feminine sexuality.

Our prime concern here, however, is not to discuss that conference or to raise the feminist issue, but to recognize that we can see, today, two different roads to worship. The first is the one we have been expounding, centered in Jesus Christ— that the triune God of grace who created us for a life of communion has redeemed us and has given himself to be known and loved as Father, Son and Holy Spirit, and has provided for us a covenanted form of worship. A New Testament understanding of worship, as we have stressed, is the gift of participating through the Spirit in the Son's communion with the Father. Here the Spirit lifts us out of any narcissistic preoccupation with ourselves to find our true humanity and dignity in Jesus Christ, in a life centered in others, in communion with Jesus Christ and one another, in a loving concern for the humanity of all. The second kind of worship is centered in the self, where we celebrate the self and our own sexuality with a god created in our own image.

This was the road taken by the ancient fertility cults in the Canaanite religion of the priests of Baal, which brought the protest of Old Testament prophets like Elijah. We can see why the Bible and the early Church had to contend against certain forms of gnosticism with its female, hermaphrodite, androgynous deities. We can understand why the Re-Imagining Conference raised many alarm bells in the American churches. Clearly, most women in our churches would not want to go to these extremes. But many might still ask why we cannot use female images for God to express his love and compassion. Some have suggested that instead of talking about "Father, Son and Holy Spirit," we talk about God as "Creator, Redeemer and Sanctifier." But this would be a new form of modalism or Sabellianism, a job description of the one God at work. It would not do justice to the personal communion between the persons of the triune God.

In the Church of Scotland, a joint Woman's Guild/Panel on Doctrine Study Group in 1984 produced a booklet entitled *The Motherhood of God*.[6] It took its stand on the doctrine of the Trinity—that Father, Son and Holy Spirit language is not negotiable. But it examined very carefully mother images used in the Bible and in the history of the Christian church—as by Julian of Norwich. They suggested that the concept of motherliness might help some people to think more about the love, tenderness and affection in God—what is revealed to us in the life, ministry and sacrifice of Jesus Christ. It was a serious way of listening to the concerns of women and the feminist movement, recognizing that in a male-dominated culture, patriarchal images and language have been too often used for God.

However, certain questions remain to be asked:

□ Does this imply that the revelation of God as Father in the person of the Son and his death on the cross for our redemption is incomplete, and that we must add motherliness to it out of our own experience?

□ Does this imply that there is gender in God, which would

clearly be false? Or again, if God is beyond gender, as we believe, is he so utterly transcendent and ineffable in his being that we ought to use both male and female images to "re-imagine God"? What does this say to us about the Christian doctrine of revelation—that "by God alone can God be known"?

☐ Would this approach really help the feminist cause? The ancient world was full of goddesses like Astarte or Aphrodite, or the female deities in Canaanite religion. But did it help women? Tragically, the deifying of sex led too often to temple prostitution as a celebration of sexuality. The Old Testament prophets of Israel were very well aware of this; and, although they could use beautiful similes of God being "like a mother," they never addressed God as "Mother."[7] I do not think this can be dismissed on the basis that they were too patriarchal! They were well aware of the dangers of the fertility cults.

☐ What is our criterion of truth? Suppose we do seek for new images of God in the depths of our experience, which is so relative to our culture and tradition. How can we decide what is right or wrong, true or false? The Motherhood of God Study Group was careful to recognize that our one true criterion is the revelation of God in Jesus Christ.

☐ What about the sources of revelation? I have heard it contended by certain radical feminists, in a college torn by this issue, that no doubt God revealed himself then in the Bible in patriarchal terms as Father, but God is revealing himself today in the feminist movement. So it was argued that if you want to call God "Father" in your own personal devotions, you may do so. But in corporate college worship with men and women together, you should avoid the words "Father" and "Son," as this is allegedly offensive to some women. Is this not a liberal Protestant form of the old Tridentine doctrine in the Roman Catholic church—of two sources of revelation, Scripture and tradition—rejected at Vatican II? There is only one source of revelation, in Jesus Christ who comes to us in Scripture and our evangelical tradition as the Lord of tradition. This relates again to the question of our criterion of truth. Is our one criterion the triune God, revealed uniquely in Jesus Christ, as in the stand taken by Athanasius and the Nicene Fathers, or are we left with only highly relative subjective criteria? Are we thrown back on ourselves to find new forms of self-expression congenial to our culture?

There is no doubt that theology matters. We are today witnessing a wave of neo-Arianism, of neo-gnosticism—in some cases the explicit identification of the self with God—the inroads of narcissistic relativism even into the life of the church. What did Jesus mean when he said, "I am the Way, the Truth and the Life; no one comes to the Father but by me" and "Anyone who has seen me has seen the Father"?

Between Scylla and Charybdis

George Carey, the Archbishop of Canterbury, in a C. S. Lewis Center Lecture delivered in 1994 at Kings College, London, spoke about the temptation of the church to succumb either to fundamentalism or postmodernism, and said the church today must chart her perilous voyage through the troublesome waters of Western culture—between Scylla and Charybdis.[8] We must contend to preserve our trinitarian faith as expressed in the Nicene Creed. This it seems to me is a timely word for all our churches.

Many churches today are polarized at one extreme or the other:

□ There is the radical liberal wing—one form of which we see in certain extreme forms of feminism. Often these militants are a minority in the life of the church, but can occupy positions of

influence and can, paradoxically, be illiberal in their use of power and their attitudes to so-called conservative evangelicals.
□ There is a rightwing conservative "fundamentalism," which can at times be legalistic in the use of Scripture, sectarian and individualistic. The latter can adopt extreme positions in reaction to what they see as the negative influence of modernism—or the relativism of postmodernism.

We can notice a number of features of so-called radical liberalism which constitute a certain progression in their line of thought, producing a conservative reaction.

1. The liberals can take a valid, relevant idea—about love or justice or male-female equality or unconditional acceptance—out of the New Testament, detach it from the person of Jesus Christ and the gospel of grace, and then attach it to the self, and fill it with their own experience as a meaningful form of self-expression. An extreme illustration in our secular society might be the actress Madonna, who takes from her Roman Catholic background the concepts of virgin and immaculate conception, detaches them from anything to do with Mary and the gospel, and uses them to celebrate her own sexuality as a sex goddess! Less extreme forms can be found in Protestantism. The conference on "Re-Imagining God, Community and the Church" might be seen in similar terms. Here the completely valid concept of male-female equality, with the concern for feminine dignity and the demand for true humanity, can be taken from the New Testament, detached from the Trinity and the incarnation, attached to feminine spirituality and made the basis for new relevant forms of worship in celebrating feminine sexuality and liberation.

The background to this can be seen in the Protestant liberal model and its presupposition that God is unknown, as it developed from Immanuel Kant, through Schleiermacher, to

Rudolf Bultmann and even to the antirealism of Don Cupitt and postmodernism. Schleiermacher's basic presupposition is that we do not know God, but he makes a valiant attempt in his theology to justify God-talk. The essence of religion is a feeling of absolute dependence on the "unknown God," the great whence and source of all. If we examine this noncognitive feeling we can reinterpret doctrines as "accounts of the religious affections set forth in speech." Therefore, the task of theology is threefold: to trace doctrines back genetically to their source in feeling, to discard all that cannot be so traced and then to interpret the rest more faithfully by the criterion of authentic self-understanding. This was the theology of romanticism, with its stress on feeling. In these terms there was for Schleiermacher no concept of an ontological Trinity, but at best the doctrine of the Trinity might be retained in Sabellian fashion as a way of describing the relationship between "the unknown God" and ourselves. Schleiermacher's pioneer work on hermeneutics, worked out in analogous fashion, was developed by Wilhelm Dilthey and applied to the interpretation of history and other human studies. This in turn lay behind Rudolf Bultmann's program of "demythologizing," his avowed concern to convert theological and christological statements into anthropological, autobiographical statements—statements about ourselves and our own self-understanding in our relation to "the unknown God." How far do we witness the same program in the call to "reimagine God" in the light of feminine self-understanding?

2. When such ideas are detached from the gospel of the incarnation and attached to ourselves, they can become the basis of an ideology, a political agenda in terms of which everything else is interpreted. What is an ideology? Sociologists point to three features: (a) it serves vested interests; (b) it interprets reality, culture, politics, the Bible, in terms of these

vested interests; (c) it is passionately believed by sincere people.

Certain forms of radical feminism, in the passionate concern for justice and liberation, can be an illustration of this. But when such an ideology is detached from Jesus Christ and the gospel of grace, it can give rise to a new legalism and a desire for power to implement its ends, using the twin tools of exhortation and condemnation (the *dikaiōmata* and *katakrimata* of the law, in Pauline terms) and lose the motivation of grace. But as Paul saw, the law, although it can expose guilty situations, never converts. It can even instigate opposition, unless it is seen as a "tutor" (*paidagōgos*) to lead us to Christ.

3. The third stage can arise when in the name of these valid and relevant ideas, the so-called liberal can then attack the gospel and reject the doctrines of the Trinity and the incarnation—the process that Michael Polanyi, in his criticism of fascism and communism, has called "moral inversion." So John Hick extracts from the New Testament the idea of love (*agapē*) to make an independent ideology, to give him a transcendental standpoint to survey world religions and engage in interreligious dialogue. But then he proceeds to attack "the myth of God incarnate" and the uniqueness of the Christian gospel.

Or again, the concept of *Sophia* (wisdom) can be lifted out of the Bible and made the basis of a new, allegedly relevant, form of feminine worship which replaces the unique place of Jesus Christ and the language of the Trinity—where milk and honey are substituted for bread and wine. Likewise, the idea of relationships of unconditional love, acceptance and forgiveness can be derived from the New Testament, detached from our acceptance in Christ, and made the basis of a new relevant approach to ethics. But then, if all that is required is love, what is the basis of a Christian doctrine of marriage or of the distinction between heterosexuality and homosexuality? Opposition to this permissive approach can then be dismissed as legalism or homophobia. In the story of the woman taken in adultery, Jesus adopted neither a legalistic nor a permissive approach, but administered grace and forgiveness. But he could also say: "Go and sin no more."

A similar approach is seen in gnosticism in its many forms down through the ages, where the idea of "the Christ" is detached from Jesus Christ, and attached to our own self-understanding, and made the basis of a religious interpretation of God. For example, in our century in Nazi Germany, the German Christians wanted a Christ who was not a Jew, so they detached the Christ from the man "Jesus the Jew," and attached the idea to themselves to worship an "Aryan Christ." In similar fashion today we witness the demand for certain forms of indigenous theology, or an Asian theology which wants to detach "the Christ" from Jesus Christ, and then attach the idea to an indigenous culture and traditional spirituality. This, of course, can be motivated by the recognition that we in the West have too often detached Jesus Christ from his roots in Israel and created a European theology and a Gentile Christ whom others do not truly recognize in the pages of the Bible. Certain radical feminists, in not dissimilar fashion, in their desire for a feminine Christ, can seek to detach the idea of "the Christ" from the man (male) Jesus, and fill the concept with their own feminine self-understanding. Others want to detach the Spirit from the Father and the Son, attach it to their own spirit, and talk about their own spirituality.

It is significant that the first epistle of John in the New Testament is already dealing with an incipient gnosticism of this kind, associated with the early gnostic Cerinthus. Hence the exhortation: "Dear friends, do not believe every spirit, but test the spirits to see whether they are of God. . . . Every spirit that acknowledges that Jesus Christ has come in the flesh is from God: but every spirit that does not acknowledge Jesus is not from God. This is the spirit of the antichrist" (4:1ff.). Again, in chapter 2, the apostle describes the antichrist as the one "who denies that Jesus is the Christ . . . he denies the Father and the Son. No one who denies the Son has the Father: whoever acknowledges the Son has the Father also" (vv. 22-23). The New Testament knows no Christ who is not Jesus Christ, the Word made flesh, and no Spirit who is not the Spirit of the Father and the Son. First John is again particularly instructive on the subject of love. The only real unconditional love (*agapē*) we know is the love of Jesus Christ revealed on the cross. "Herein is love, not that we loved God but that he loved us and sent his Son to be the propitiation for our sins" (4:7ff.). It is with that love, defined for us by Jesus Christ and his love, and shed abroad in our hearts by the Holy Spirit, that we are summoned to love and accept and forgive one another unconditionally. Our loving communion with one another is the gift of participating together, through the Spirit, in Christ's ministry of reconciling love in the community of men and women.

4. The next stage in this liberal progression is to call in question the authority of the Bible. This might be done by asserting that the Bible is a manual of patriarchy, the product of a male-dominated culture, or outdated, for example, in its primitive views on and condemnation of homosexuality. Of course the Bible can be used to justify patriarchy, slavery, racism, sexism, but for this very reason we must all the more interpret the Bible in terms of its fulfillment in Jesus Christ. He liberates us from false prejudice, and summons us to reject slavery, racism, sexism and patriarchy in his work of redeeming our fallen race and bringing in the new creation. What was lost in fallen Adam is restored in Christ. In this way the gospel is

meant, in speaking to culture, to transform culture.

5. A final stage might be the one we have already referred to, of questioning the sole authority of the Bible by teaching a doctrine of two sources—the Bible and tradition—that God without doubt revealed himself long ago in a primitive patriarchal culture, but is progressively revealing himself today in our more enlightened culture, eclipsing earlier revelations of himself.

This whole liberal progression can lead in reaction to a rightwing conservative "fundamentalism" in an understandable concern to stand upon the authority of the Bible. It can sometimes lead to wrong legalistic uses of the Bible and, in a way not totally dissimilar to liberalism, fail to interpret the Bible christologically. This, further coupled with an inward-looking individualistic pietism, can too easily turn a blind eye to the social issues of our time and a deaf ear to the cries for justice and liberty in our contemporary society. As we stressed earlier, in witnessing to Jesus Christ today there should be no divorce between evangelism and humanization.

What do we learn from all this? So many churches today are sadly polarized at one or the other of these two extremes. In some ways, they can have much in common. Both can make experience their criterion. The liberals appeal to contemporary self-understanding or self-expression in formulating their ideology. The conservatives appeal to "evangelical experience," as in the existential experience model. Where the one group, by selecting certain relevant ideas and abstracting them from the gospel, can detach them from the person of Jesus Christ, the other can sometimes so identify faith with subscription to orthodox doctrines that they can substitute abstract dogmas for the living person of Jesus Christ, and make subscription to doctrines a condition of acceptance—as in sectarianism, be it

Catholic or Protestant.

In steering our way between Scylla and Charybdis (to adopt the Archbishop of Canterbury's metaphor), we need to remind ourselves constantly that the center of the church is not ourselves, but Jesus Christ, our living Lord. Under the pressures of our culture, and of theological controversy, are we not in danger of losing that living center—of forgetting that the real agent in the life of the church is not ourselves, but Jesus Christ? Then our worship becomes in practice unitarian and Pelagian, simply what we, religious people, do. It is no longer seen as participating by grace through the Spirit in the incarnate Son's communion with the Father. The Eucharist is no longer central.

Already in the New Testament, we can see that there was the temptation for the Church to lose that living center, by taking her eyes off Jesus Christ. That is the basic theme of Paul's letters to the Corinthians. By taking their eyes off "Christ and him crucified," the gospel which Paul had preached to them, they landed up in divisions and quarrels about spirituality and coveted one another's gifts. It is also the basic theme of the epistle to the Hebrews, with its emphasis on the sole priesthood of Christ, who alone, by his atoning death for our sin, can lead us into the Holy of Holies—the holy presence of the Father. Jesus Christ is the true leader of our worship, and if we take our eyes off him we fall back on ourselves, with a false confidence in the flesh, in what we do, in a religion which can never take away sins or lead us into true communion with God. We fall back into unbelief. We commented in our second chapter on the context of the epistle.[9] It is worth considering it again, as it is so relevant in our own day. It was written to Christians who had steadily declined from their early commitment to Christ. Those who had once led them to Christ were now dead. Without their encouragement, they had lost their early faith and zeal. Where they themselves should have gone on to spiritual maturity, to be leaders and teachers (5:12), they had backslidden, and needed someone to teach them the first principles of the faith (5:12-14). They were like the people of Israel in the wilderness who rebelled against Moses, under whom God had brought them out of Egypt, and so were unable to enter into the promised land because of their unbelief. They had gone back to their old ways and were in danger of apostasy (6:9; 10:35). By taking their eyes off Christ, their worship had degenerated into a matter of "food and drink and various ceremonial washings, of external rules and regulations which could never clear the conscience of the worshiper—'the ordinances of the flesh' " (*dikaiōmata sarkos*) (9:9-10). It was the road to spiritual death. So the author, after citing the examples of the great men and women of faith in their history—"a great cloud of witnesses"—exhorts them to run with perseverance the way set before them. "Let us fix our eyes on Jesus, the author and the perfecter of our faith, who for the joy set before him endured the cross, scorning its shame, and sat down at the right hand of God" (12:1-3). "Therefore, brothers (and sisters), who share in the heavenly calling, fix your thoughts on Jesus, the apostle and high priest whom we confess" (3:1). Only in this way could they discover again the joy of true worship. So the epistle speaks about the high priesthood of Christ, who died once and for all to wipe out our sins, and who now as their reigning Lord "ever lives to make intercession for us"—to lead us into the presence of God.

The epistle has so much to say to us about true worship and the place of Jesus Christ in our worship and prayer life today. By our divisions and polarization between so-called liberalism and fundamentalism are we not in danger of losing that living center? Our risen ascended Lord, the head of the church, summons us to look to him, to remember his sacrifice for us on the cross that we might receive the forgiveness of our sins, that he might lead us to the Father, lifting us up by the Spirit to share his life of communion with the Father in communion with one another, that we might feed upon him, the bread of life. Is this not the meaning of Holy Communion? Our high priest has passed into the heavens, not to leave us outside like the people in Old Testament Israel on the Day of Atonement, but to take us with himself into the Holy of Holies. As we look to him in faith, we know that the righteous requirements (*dikaiōmata*) of the law and the ordinances of worship have not only been fulfilled for us by Christ, but are fulfilled in us as we live in the Spirit (Rom 8:1-4). By him the love of God is shed abroad in our hearts—the Spirit by whom we cry, "*Abba*, Father," who intercedes for us and in us when we do not know how to pray as we ought (vv. 26-27).

But if we take our eyes off Christ, like those to whom the epistle to the Hebrews was written, we fall back on ourselves with a false "self-confidence in the flesh" that we can keep the ordinances of worship (*dikaiōmata latreias*, Heb 9:1) by our religion, that we can offer worthy worship to God and meet his holy requirements. That is the road to apostasy, to sectarian divisions, to legalism, to weariness, where religion becomes a "yoke grievous to be borne." Then people will drift away from the church, we shall lose our young people who will want to cast off the "yoke," and our members will lose the motivation of grace to give time and service and money to the church. That road can lead in the end to false worship, or even in our pagan society to the worship of Mammon or sex or self—our modern counterparts to the golden calf, the nature gods of the Baalim and the fertility cults. Or it can lead us simply to unbelief, apathy or even despair. "There is a way that seems right to a man, but in the end it leads to death" (Prov 14:12). Jesus said, "I am the Way and the Truth and the Life. No one comes to the Father except through me." Let us look to him and his Spirit will lift us up as a community of faith into the very triune life of God. He is doing that for you now. God bless you!

Appendix

On Human Language for God

Simile, Metaphor, Parable, Analogy, Name

THE BIBLE DOES USE FEMALE IMAGES AND PARABLES for God and the kingdom of God, but it uses them as similes, not as metaphors.[1] When we say, "God is like a shepherd," that is a simile, but when we say, "The Lord is my shepherd," that is metaphor. A metaphor is a word (noun) with a dictionary meaning, boldly transferred to something or someone else to show significance and provide new understanding (e.g., shepherd, Lamb of God, "I am the door"). The biblical writers do not use mother as a metaphor for God. They never addressed God as "Mother." They were too aware of the feminine deities of the fertility cults, Astarte or Aphrodite, and indeed of the danger of making any images of God, as in the prohibition of the Second Commandment: "You saw no form of any kind the day the Lord spoke to you in Horeb out of the fire. Therefore take good heed to yourselves, so that you do not become corrupt by making a graven image for yourselves, whether formed like a man or a woman" (Deut 4:15-16). Again the people are reminded: "God is not a man" (Num 23:19). In only four passages in the Old Testament is the *simile* of motherhood used of God:

❑ "For a long time I have kept silent. I have been quiet and held myself back. But now, like a woman in childbirth, I cry out, I gasp and pant" (Is 42:14).

❑ "Woe to him who quarrels with his Maker. Woe to him who says to his father, 'What have you begotten?' or to his mother, 'What have you brought to birth?' " (Is 45:9-10).

❑ "Can a mother forget the baby at her breast and have no compassion on the child she has borne? Though she may forget, I will not forget you!" (Is 49:15).

❑ "As a mother comforts her child, so will I comfort you" (Is 66:13).

These are similes, not metaphors. There is no assertion of any motherhood in God, but certain attributes of a woman are used to speak about the attributes of love and compassion in God. In similar fashion, the word *Sophia* (wisdom) is used to describe an attribute in God, or the wise purposes of God. There is a certain personification of wisdom in Proverbs 8. But *Sophia* is not literally a person to be personally addressed.

What then about the word "Father" when God is addressed as Father? Is this just another metaphor for God, like "shepherd"? Clearly God is not really a shepherd, although it is a meaningful word. Do we then say that God is not really Father, but this is a meaningful form of address? Is not God more truly Father than we human fathers are? Clearly, much depends on how we interpret metaphor. There have been many discussions about this, some saying that Father, unlike rock or shepherd, is a "reality depicting metaphor."[2] The word denotes personal identity in God, not just certain fatherly attributes, in virtue of which we can address him as "Father."

Perhaps it is better to talk about *analogy*. The word "father" is truly predicated of God and of creatures, but analogically. God has revealed himself to us as Father. He has not left himself to be unknown. But the word is not just a model, a metaphor which *we* use to describe God—"reality depicting" as such a metaphor might be. God has *named* himself as "Father." A name is more than a metaphor. In naming himself, God has commandeered human language to reveal himself. We only know human fathers. For us the word "father" is a human class concept, which we predicate of creaturely male parents. How then can a word which is a human class concept be used to denote God who is not a member of that class? How can we use a word with sexual connotations to denote God who is beyond gender? How can fatherhood then be predicated of God and man? Clearly not univocally, with identity of meaning. That would certainly imply gender in God.[3] If the human word "father" is to be used of God, there must be a shift in meaning to denote God the Creator, who is the only true Father, after whom all earthly fatherhood is named (Eph 3:15). In the order of being, God's fatherhood is prior to ours, as the creator is prior to the creature. However, in the order of knowing, we know earthly fathers before we know God as Father. How then can we compare and contrast God's fatherhood with ours? We can only do so theologically (not mythologically, to refer again to Athanasius's distinction) by the content put into that word by Jesus Christ, as we reflect upon the life of Jesus, the words of Jesus, the sufferings of Jesus.[4] We allow the Spirit, in interpreting Christ to us, to evacuate the word of all biological, male, patriarchal, sexist content, to fill it with divine content, that we may more truly pray, "*Abba*, Father." This is the road of analogy (*analogia gratiae*) in theology. The presupposition of this, as the Nicene Fathers saw, is that the Father and the Son are "one in being" (*homoousioi*): "He who has seen me has seen the Father" (Mt 11:27; Jn 14:9). In similar fashion the relational words "person" and "communion," like "love" (*agapē*), are predicated of God and humanity, not mythologically but theologically, in the light of the revelation of God in Jesus Christ. It was in this way that the fathers of the church taught the doctrine of an ontological Trinity—that the God who has his being-in-communion, in love, has created us as human persons in his image to find our true being-in-communion in love, in perichoretic unity, and revealed that purpose to us in Jesus Christ.

The concept of the name of God—that God names himself—occurs all through the Bible. In redeeming Israel from Egypt, God gave his name to Moses: "I am who I am. This is my name forever, the name by which I am to be remembered from generation to generation" (Ex 3:15). "My people will know my name" (as their redeemer) (Is 52:6). "The Lord your God will choose a dwelling place for his name" (Deut 12:11). In pronouncing the Aaronic blessing of peace at the conclusion of worship, the priests "will put my name on the Israelites" (Num 6:27; cf. Ps 20:1, 5; 54:1; 124:8; Jer 23:6). In the New Testament, the God who gave his name to Israel, in the fulfillment of his revelation, makes his name known as "Father" in Jesus, and gave to his Son Jesus a name above every name. Jesus himself prayed, "Father, glorify your name" (Jn 12:28) and taught us to pray, "Hallowed be your name." In our Lord's high priestly prayer, he says: "I am coming to you, Holy Father; protect them by the power of your name—the name you gave me—so that they may be one as we are one. While I was with them I protected them and kept them safe by that name you gave me" (Jn 17:11-12). We are baptized into the name of the Father, Son and Holy Spirit, and are taught to confess it, praise it, love it, proclaim it, in a life of wonderful communion. It should be clear from all that we have said, therefore, that the name is not merely an arbitrary signifier, like Susan or Fred! It has semantic content, as has the name of Jesus. It is the name through which God discloses himself personally to us to draw us into intimate communion with himself in worship and prayer, not just to convey information about himself.

Notes

Chapter 1: Worship—Unitarian or Trinitarian?

[1]See my chapter on "The Vicarious Humanity of Christ" in *The Incarnation*, ed. T. F. Torrance (Edinburgh: Handsel Press, 1981); also on "The Doctrine of the Trinity in our Contemporary Situation" in *The Forgotten Trinity*, vol. 3 (London: British Council of Churches, 1991).

[2]See D. Butler, *Henry Scougal and the Oxford Methodists* (Edinburgh & London: Wm. Blackwood & Sons, 1899).

[3]Adolf Harnack, *What is Christianity?* (New York: Harper, 1957), pp. 144ff.

[4]Ibid., p. 142.

[5]She interpreted life in heaven not just in terms of the beatific vision of beauty, truth and goodness, but as one of eternal worship, understood in trinitarian terms. (Julian of Norwich, *Showings*, in The Classics of Western Spirituality, trans. Colledge and Walsh (New York: Paulist Press, 1978), p. 81.) Cf. James M. Houston, "Spirituality and the Doctrine of the Trinity," and Roland Walls, "The Church: a Communion of Persons" (on Julian of Norwich), in *Christ in Our Place: The Humanity of God in Christ for the Reconciliation of the World* (Exeter: Paternoster Press, 1990).

[6]This is why the recent discussions among the churches on "the *filioque* clause" (that the Spirit proceeds from the Father "and the Son") require to be set in the larger context of a full discussion of the Trinity, as it emerges out of a scrutiny of the Church's worship. Whether or not we subscribe to the Western *filioque*, the fundamental question is how to understand the relationship of the Spirit to him who is the Father of the Son and to him who is the Son of the Father. In the Spirit, the one triune God is giving himself to us in grace to draw us into a life of communion in the fulfillment of his purposes for us in creation.

[7]*The Forgotten Trinity* (London: British Council of Churches, 1989-91).

[8]See my discussion of this in "Covenant or Contract? A Study of the Theological Background of Worship in Seventeenth Century Scotland," *Scottish Journal of Theology* 23 (1970): 51-76. Also "The Covenant Concept in Scottish Theology and Politics and Its Legacy," *Scottish Journal of Theology* 34 (1981): 225-43.

[9]See also my articles "Covenant or Contract?" and "The Covenant Concept in Scottish Theology and Politics and Its Legacy."

[10]See John Macmurray, *Reason and Emotion* (London: Faber & Faber, 1935).

[11]John Zizioulas, *Being as Communion* (London: Darton, Longman & Todd, 1985). John Macmurray, *Persons in Relation* (London: Faber & Faber, 1961). John Macmurray, *The Self as Agent* (London: Faber & Faber, 1957). See also Walls, "The Church: A Communion of Persons," in *Christ in Our Place.*

[12]Allan Bloom, *The Closing of the American Mind* (New York: Simon & Schuster, 1987).

[13]See also David Lyon, *Postmodernity* (Buckingham: Open University Press, 1994).

Chapter 2: The Sole Priesthood of Christ

[1]Cf. Columba Marmion, *Christ in His Mysteries* (London: Sands & Co., 1939); Calvin *Institutes* 4.17.2.

[2]For a discussion of the significance of the one and the many for our understanding of worship and the doctrine of the church, see A. Michael Ramsey, *The Gospel and the Catholic Church* (London: Longmans, Green & Co., 1936). Also Colin E. Gunton, *The One, the Three and the Many* (Cambridge: Cambridge University Press, 1993).

[3]Calvin, *Commentary on Hebrews* 6:19, CO55-81. See my discussion of this, International Congress on Calvin Research, "The Vicarious Humanity and Priesthood of Christ in the Theology of John Calvin," in *Calvinus Ecclesiae Doctor* (Kampen: J. H. Kok, 1978).

[4]This is the passage to which John Duns Scotus appealed in speaking about the immaculate conception of Mary. She was immaculate *in the person of her Son.* She was a member of the fallen human race, elected by God to be the mother of our Lord, redeemed ("preredeemed") and cleansed by the blood of her Son. As such she is a symbol of the church of the redeemed. See my discussion of right ways and wrong ways of interpreting this in Roman Catholic history in James B. Torrance and Roland C. Walls, *John Duns Scotus in a Nutshell* (Edinburgh: Handsel Press, 1992). Here it seems to me Duns Scotus was a forerunner of Calvin, through the influence of John Major in Paris, and often misinterpreted. The church of the redeemed is immaculate in Christ, not in herself.

[5]Calvin *Institutes* 3.11-14.

[6]E.g., Gregory of Nazianzus *Epistles* 101. See T. F. Torrance, *Theology in Reconciliation* (London: Geoffrey Chapman, 1975), pp. 112, 154, 167.

[7]See my discussion of this in International Congress on Calvin Research, "The Meaning of Grace in Calvin . . . Salvation Complete in Christ," in *Calvinus Sacrae Scripturae Professor* (Grand Rapids: Eerdmans, 1990), pp. 12ff. Also in *Calvinus Ecclesiae Doctor.*

[8]Calvin *Institutes* 3.4.

[9]See my discussion of this in "The Vicarious Humanity of Christ," in *The*

Incarnation: Ecumenical Studies in the Nicene-Constantinopolitan Creed, AD 381, ed. Thomas F. Torrance (Edinburgh: Handsel Press, 1981). Also in "The Contribution of John McLeod Campbell to Scottish Theology," *Scottish Journal of Theology* 26 (1973).

[10]No one saw this more clearly than John Calvin in his exposition of the worship of Old Testament Israel. See T. F. Torrance's discussion of this in "The Mediation of Christ in Our Human Response," in *The Mediation of Christ*, revised edition (Edinburgh: T & T Clark, 1992).

[11]J. Jungmann, *The Place of Christ in Liturgical Prayer* (London and Dublin: Chapman, 1965).

Chapter 3: Baptism & the Lord's Supper—the Way of Communion

[1]Dietrich Bonhoeffer, *Christology*, ET (London: Collins; New York: Harper & Row, 1966).

[2]James B. Torrance and Roland C. Walls, *John Duns Scotus in a Nutshell* (Edinburgh: Handsel Press, 1992).

[3]Oscar Cullmann, cited in *Doctrine and Practice of Public Worship in the Reformed Churches*, a report to the General Assembly of the Church of Scotland, 1971.

[4]J. K. S. Reid, *Church Service Society Annual*, May 1960, p. 10.

[5]See an engaging discussion of this in M. V. Bernadot, O.P., *The Eucharist and the Trinity* (Wilmington, Del.: Michael Glazier, 1977). (Originally published by Sands & Co. as *From Holy Communion to the Holy Trinity*, trans. from the French.)

Chapter 4: Gender, Sexuality & the Trinity

[1]Athanasius used this distinction in his earliest works, even before the Arian controversy, e.g., *Contra Gentes* 19. For a discussion of this distinction, see T. F. Torrance, *Theology in Reconstruction* (London: SCM, 1963), pp. 34ff., 46ff.

[2]See Appendix.

[3]This is Daphne Hampson's contention in *Theology and Feminism* (Oxford: Blackwell, 1990).

[4]See my chapter, "The Contribution of John Duns Scotus to the Theology of a Christian Church," in James B. Torrance and Roland C. Walls, *John Duns Scotus in a Nutshell* (Edinburgh: Handsel Press, 1992).

[5]V. Norskov Olsen, *The New Relatedness for Man and Woman in Christ: A Mirror of the Divine* (Riverside, Calif.: Loma Linda University Press, 1993), where there is an excellent discussion of male-female relations in the light of relatedness in the triune God, of "headship" in the Pauline Letters, and also of the context of 1 Timothy 2 where the apostle does not allow women to usurp authority (*authentein*) in the church, as in certain female gnostic sects. In such a sect in Ephesus there was apparently a goddess Authentia. See also my introduction to this book.

[6]Alan E. Lewis, ed., *The Motherhood of God* (Edinburgh: St. Andrew Press, 1984).

[7]See Appendix.

[8]A summary of his lecture appeared in *Leading Light* 2/1, Winter 1995, the journal of Gospel and Culture.

[9]See the excellent study of this epistle in J. G. S. S. Thompson, *The Praying Christ* (London: Tyndale Press; Grand Rapids: Eerdmans, 1954), especially chapter five, "A Merciful and Faithful High Priest."

Appendix: On Human Language for God

[1]See the discussion on this in Roland M. Frye, *Language for God and Feminist Language* (Edinburgh: Handsel Press, 1988).

[2]Janet Martin Soskice, *Metaphor and Religious Language* (Oxford: Clarendon, 1985). Sallie McFague, *Metaphorical Theology: Models of God in Religious Language* (London: SCM, 1982).

[3]As Aquinas saw, when we say "God is not in any class" (*deus non est in genere*), to predicate fatherhood of God and man analogically is clearly not a case of an *analogia generis—analogia duorum ad tertium*—that God and man are subsumed under a third thing, a general class concept, in some general *analogia entis*. It is rather a case of *analogia unius ad alterum* ("of one to another")—between God and the creature, where God is the *analogia analogans*, the ground of the analogy, and the creaturely father is the *analogia analogata*, the analogate (what Karl Barth saw must be interpreted as an *analogia gratiae* or *analogia relationis*, an *analogia fidei*). To invert the order and make the creaturely father the *analogia analogans*, the ground of the analogy, is the road of mythology or a crude anthropomorphism (to treat God as a passionate old man like Father Zeus in Greek mythology!). This is the danger in calling for new human images of God, be they male or female. See Battista Mondin, *The Principle of Analogy in Protestant and Catholic Theology* (The Hague: Martinus Nijhoff, 1963).

[4]In analogy, we compare and contrast the terms, seeing likeness and unlikeness (steering our way, as Aquinas saw, between a *via negativa* and a *via affirmativa*). So we sing with Frederick Faber:

No earthly father loves like thee;
No mother e'er so mild
Bears and forebears as thou hast done
With me thy sinful child.

There is a "cloud of unknowing." Yet the light of the Father's love shines through the darkness of the cross. True theology is theology that sings:

Yet I may love thee too, O Lord,
Almighty as thou art,
For thou hast stooped to ask of me
The love of my poor heart.